ALSO BY GEORGE LAKOFF

Don't Think of an Elephant!
Know Your Values and Frame the Debate

Moral Politics: How Liberals and Conservatives Think

Metaphors We Live By

More Than Cool Reason: A Field Guide to Poetic Metaphor

Women, Fire, and Dangerous Things:
What Categories Reveal About the Mind

Philosophy in the Flesh:
The Embodied Mind and Its Challenge to Western Thought

Where Mathematics Comes From:
How the Embodied Mind Brings Mathematics into Being

WHOSE FREEDOM?

WHOSE FREEDOM?

THE BATTLE OVER AMERICA'S

MOST IMPORTANT IDEA

———◆———

GEORGE LAKOFF

FARRAR, STRAUS AND GIROUX / NEW YORK

Farrar, Straus and Giroux
19 Union Square West, New York 10003

Distributed in Canada by Douglas & McIntyre Ltd.
Printed in the United States of America
First edition, 2006

Library of Congress Cataloging-in-Publication Data
Lakoff, George.
    Whose freedom? : the battle over America's most important idea /
George Lakoff.— 1st ed.
        p.   cm.
    ISBN-13: 978-0-374-15828-6 (hardcover : alk. paper)
    ISBN-10: 0-374-15828-2 (hardcover : alk. paper)
    1. Liberty—United States. 2. Conservatism—United States.
3. Progressivism (United States politics) 4. United States—Politics
and government—2001–   I. Title.

JC599.U5L25 2006
323.440973—dc22

                                                    2006004265

Designed by Jonathan D. Lippincott

www.fsgbooks.com

1   3   5   7   9   10   8   6   4   2

To Kathleen

CONTENTS

Introduction: In the Name of Freedom   3

PART I: UNCONTESTED FREEDOM
1 Freedom Is Freedom Is Freedom   21
2 Why Freedom Is Visceral   28
3 The Logic of Simple Freedom   39

PART II: CONTESTED FREEDOM
4 The Nation-as-Family Metaphor   65
5 Progressive Freedom: The Basics   73
6 Conservative Freedom: The Basics   95
7 Causation and Freedom   111

PART III: FORMS OF FREEDOM
8 Personal Freedom and Populism   133
9 Economic Freedom   149
10 Religion and Freedom   170
11 Foreign Policy and Freedom   202

PART IV: IDEAS AND ACTION
12 Bush's "Freedom"   229
13 Taking Back Freedom   243

Suggested Reading   267
Acknowledgments   275

WHOSE FREEDOM?

INTRODUCTION:
IN THE NAME OF FREEDOM

Ideas matter. Perhaps no idea has mattered more in American history than the idea of freedom.

The central thesis of this book is simple. There are two very different views of freedom in America today, arising from two very different moral and political worldviews dividing the country.

The traditional idea of freedom is progressive. One can see traditional values most clearly in the direction of change that has been demanded and applauded over two centuries. America has been a nation of activists, consistently expanding its most treasured freedoms:

- The expansion of citizen participation and voting rights from white male property owners to non–property owners, to former slaves, to women, to those excluded by prejudice, to younger voters
- The expansion of opportunity, good jobs, better working conditions, and benefits to more and more Americans, from men to women, from white to nonwhite, from native born to foreign born, from English speaking to non–English speaking
- The expansion of worker rights—freedom from inhumane working conditions—through unionization: from slave labor to the eight-hour day, the five-day week,

worker compensation, sick leave, overtime pay, paid vacations, pregnancy leave, and so on
- The expansion of public education from grade school to high school to college to postgraduate education
- The expansion of knowledge through science from isolated figures like Benjamin Franklin to scientific institutions in the great universities and governmental institutions like the National Science Foundation and the National Institutes of Health
- The expansion of public health and life expectancy
- The expansion of consumer protection through more effective government regulation of immoral or irresponsible corporations and class action suits within the civil justice system
- The expansion of diverse media and free speech from small newspapers to the vast media/Internet possibilities of today
- The expansion of access to capital from wealthy landholders and bankers to all the ways ordinary people— more and more of them—can borrow money today
- The expansion, throughout the world, of freedom from colonial rule—for the most part with the backing of American foreign policy

These are among the progressive trends in American history. Progress has not always been linear, and the stages have been far from perfect, but the trends have been there—until recently. The rise of radical conservatism in America threatens to stop and reverse these and other progressive trends together with the progressive ideal of freedom that has propelled them all.

Indeed, the reversal has proceeded at a rapid pace. Voting rights are being threatened, good-paying jobs eliminated or exported, benefits cut or eliminated. Public education is being gutted and science is under attack. The media is being consolidated, corporate regulations eliminated, the civil justice system threatened, public health programs cut. Unions are being destroyed and benefits taken away. There are new bankruptcy laws limiting access to capital for ordinary people. And we are seeing the promotion of a new form of free-market colonialism in the guise of free-trade agreements and globalization, and even the use of military force to support these policies.

But for radical conservatives, these developments are not movements away from freedom but toward their version of freedom. Where most Americans in the last century have seen an expansion of freedoms, these conservatives see curtailments of what they consider "freedom." What makes them "conservatives" is not that they want to conserve the achievements of those who fought to deepen American democracy. It's the reverse: They want to go back to before these progressive freedoms were established. What they want to conserve is, in most cases, the situation prior to the expansion of traditional American ideas of freedom: before the great expansion of voting rights, before unions and worker protections and pensions, before civil rights legislation, before public health and environmental protections, before Social Security and Medicare, before scientific discoveries contradicted fundamentalist religious dogma. That is why they harp so much on narrow so-called originalist readings of the Constitution—on its letter, not its spirit—on "activist judges" rather than an inherently activist population.

We will be asking three questions:

- *How* are radical conservatives achieving their reversal of freedom?
- *Why* do they want to reverse traditional freedoms?
- *What* do they mean by "freedom"?

Freedom defines what America is—and it is now up for grabs. The radical right is in the process of redefining the very idea. To lose freedom is a terrible thing; to lose the idea of freedom is even worse.

The constant repetition of the words "liberty" and "freedom" by the right-wing message machine is one of the mechanisms of the idea theft in progress. When the words are used by the right, their meaning shifts—gradually, almost imperceptibly, but it shifts.

The speeches at the 2004 Republican National Convention constantly invoked the words "freedom," "free," and "liberty." George W. Bush, in his second inaugural address, used these words forty-nine times in a twenty-minute speech—every forty-third word. And if you take into account the opposites—"tyranny," "dictatorship," "slavery," and so on—as well as associated words like "democracy," the proportion rises higher. From freedom fries to the Freedom Film Festival, the right wing is claiming the words "liberty" and "freedom" as their brand: Jerry Falwell's *National Liberty Journal*, Liberty University, Liberty Counsel, Operations Iraqi Freedom and Enduring Freedom, and the list goes on.

To many progressives, the right's use of "freedom" is pure hypocrisy, and George W. Bush is the leading hypocrite. How, liberals ask, can Bush mean anything at all by "freedom" when he imprisons hundreds of people in Guantánamo indefinitely with no due process in the name of freedom; when he sanctions torture in the name of freedom; when he starts a preemptive war on false premises and retroactively claims it is being waged in the name of freedom; when he causes the deaths of tens of thousands of innocent Iraqi civilians in the name of freedom; when he supports oppressive regimes in Saudi Arabia, Egypt, and Pakistan, while claiming to promote freedom in the Islamic world; when he sanctions the disenfranchisement of African-American voters in Florida and Ohio in the name of freedom; when he orders spying on American citizens in America without a warrant in the name of freedom; when, in the name of freedom, he seeks to prevent women from making their own medical decisions, to stop loving couples who want to marry, to stop families from being able to remove life supports when their loved ones are all but technically dead.

How can Bush mean anything by "freedom" when he works against Franklin Delano Roosevelt's four freedoms: freedom of speech and religion and freedom from want and fear? His policies work against freedom from want by pushing more Americans into poverty, by denying even a minuscule increase in the minimum wage, by seeking to end Social Security. By promoting a siege mentality—announcing orange alerts and talking relentlessly about "terror"—he creates and maintains a sense of fear, virtually a permanent state of emergency, rather then offering freedom from fear. The U.S.A. Patriot Act, passed at the height of this fear, provides new police powers to the government, abridging personal freedoms. He works against freedom of speech by encouraging media consolidation, by spying on telephone calls, by having the IRS threaten the tax status of groups that speak out against him, by requiring all attendees at his public speeches to sign oaths of loyalty to him, and by classifying more government documents than any other recent administration. He works against freedom of the press by secretly paying journalists to promote his policies and by denying access to reporters who criticize his policies. And he works against freedom of religion by seeking to impose school prayer upon those who don't want to pray, by allowing federal funds to be used to promote one religion (Christianity), by tacit support of bringing a religious idea—"intelligent design"—into the classroom, and by pushing faith-based governmental programs of all kinds, programs that put taxpayer money and social control into the hands of churches approved by his administration. How, progressives ask, can he possibly mean what he says when he claims that such actions promote "freedom"? The conclusion of many progressives is that the use of the word in the face of these policies tends to make the word meaningless.

Yes, Bush's acts do contradict the progressive idea of freedom—
my idea of freedom. But progressives are engaging in fantasy
when they assume that their idea of freedom is the only possible
one and thereby deny that the radical right has any idea at all of
freedom. This form of denial results in the view that Bush is saying nothing when he speaks of "freedom," that he is just degrading the language, that he is no more than a cynical and
opportunistic propagandist who doesn't mean what he says.

In thinking this way, progressives are blinding themselves to
the real and constant progress by the radical right toward cultural and political domination. It is tempting to dismiss Bush and
members of the radical right as liars and hypocrites—but this is
too easy. It is much scarier to think of Bush and others on the
right as meaning what they say—as having a concept of "freedom" so alien to progressives that many progressives cannot even
understand it, much less defend against it. Even more troubling
is that the right's gradual takeover of the idea of freedom is going
by unnoticed by a great many people.

Most Americans believe that "freedom" has only one meaning. It serves the purposes of the right when the public believes
that conservatives and progressives are using the same idea, dis-
agreeing only over which side is its more vigorous champion. It
serves the purposes of the right to say that there is no theft, not
even a challenge, going on. The longer the attempted theft remains invisible, the better its chance of succeeding.

Even Democrats with impeccable liberal credentials are helping the radical right by engaging in denial. I was a guest on an
NPR program just after Bush's second inaugural, discussing the
remarkable repetition of the word "freedom" in the speech. The
guest who followed me was the brilliant and articulate Elaine
Kamarck, an important figure in the Clinton administration,
now at Harvard's Kennedy School of Government. She denied
that there was, or could be, more than one meaning of freedom.
"Freedom is freedom is freedom," she declared with utter assur-

ance, echoing Gertrude Stein's "A rose is a rose is a rose." The right-wing talk-show host Rush Limbaugh soon echoed Kamarck: There's one idea of freedom and only one. If Bush-Limbaugh freedom is the only idea of freedom in America, then the radical right has won.

But they have not won, not yet!

If they had won, if freedom had been redefined throughout America in their terms, if our freedom were gone and theirs were in its place, then there would be no need for them to repeat the word over and over and over. The point of repetition is to change not just people's minds but also their very brains. If they had succeeded in getting their view of freedom into the brains of all, or even most, Americans, then they could simply take freedom as they define it for granted.

THE MIND AND FREEDOM

I will be approaching the idea of freedom from the perspective of cognitive science—the interdisciplinary study of mind.

There are many excellent books on freedom written from various intellectual perspectives: intellectual history, political science, public policy, sociology, law, philosophy. The history of attempts to understand the idea of freedom has a great deal to teach us, and I am deeply grateful for the important scholarship in these areas. Nonetheless, these studies have limitations. Freedom and other political ideas are products of the human mind. They are inescapably the results of human mental processes. Cognitive science and cognitive linguistics, as these fields have developed in the past three decades, have given us a new and deeper understanding of mental processes and the ideas they generate, including political ideas.

Cognitive science has produced a number of dramatic and

important results—results that bear centrally on contemporary politics, though in a way that is not immediately obvious.

- *We think with our brains.*

The concepts we think with are physically instantiated in the synapses and neural circuitry of our brains. Thought is physical. And neural circuits, once established, do not change quickly or easily.

- *Repetition of language has the power to change brains.*

When a word or phrase is repeated over and over for a long period of time, the neural circuits that compute its meaning are activated repeatedly in the brain. As the neurons in those circuits fire, the synapses connecting the neurons in the circuits get stronger and the circuits may eventually become permanent, which happens when you learn the meaning of any word in your fixed vocabulary. Learning a word physically changes your brain, and the meaning of that word becomes physically instantiated in your brain.

For example, the word "freedom," if repeatedly associated with radical conservative themes, may be learned not with its traditional progressive meaning, but with a radical conservative meaning. "Freedom" is being redefined brain by brain.

- *Most thought is unconscious.*

Because thought occurs at the neural level, most of our thinking is not available to conscious introspection. Thus, you may not know your own reasoning processes. For example, you may not be aware of the moral or political principles that lie behind the political conclusions that you reach quickly and automatically.

- *All thought uses conceptual frames.*

"Frames" are mental structures of limited scope, with a systematic internal organization. For example, our simple frame for "war" includes semantic roles: the countries at war, their leaders, their armies, with soldiers and commanders, weapons, attacks, and battlefields. The frame includes specific knowledge: In the United States, the president is the commander in chief and has war powers; war's purpose is to protect the country; the war is over and won when the other army surrenders. All words are defined with respect to frames.

Thus, declaring a "war on terror" against an elusive and amorphous enemy gave President Bush special war powers that could be extended and used indefinitely, even against American citizens. The Iraq War framed Iraq as a threat to our nation, making anyone against the war a traitor; when the United States marched into Baghdad, the war frame said the war was over—"Mission Accomplished."

- *Frames have boundaries.*
Iraqi soldiers, tanks, and planes, and Iraq's leader, Saddam Hussein, were inside the war frame, since they fit the semantic roles of the frame. Outside the war frame were ordinary Iraqis—killed and maimed by the tens of thousands—the resentment in Iraqi families caused by those deaths and maimings, the damage to the Iraqi infrastructure, the Iraqi jobs lost because of that damage, the resistance to the American occupation, Iraqi culture and religion, the "insurgents," the ancient artifacts in the Iraqi museums, the relatives of American soldiers, American social programs cut, the mounting American deficit, the attitudes toward Americans around the world. When you think within a frame, you tend to ignore what is outside the frame.

- *Language can be used to reframe a situation.*
The Bush administration first framed the Iraq War as "regime change," as though the country would remain intact except for who ran the government. Saddam Hussein would "fall"—symbolized by his statue falling, an image played over and over on American TV—and a new democratic government would immediately

replace the old tyranny. As the insurgency began to emerge, it became clear that the old frame was inoperative, and a reframing took place: Iraq became "the main front in the war on terror."

Fox News used the headline "War on Terror" whenever footage of the insurgency was shown. During the 2004 election, Republicans were advised not to say "Iraq War" but to use "war on terror" instead, whenever possible. At the time of the election, three out of four Bush supporters believed that Saddam Hussein had given "substantial support" to al-Qaeda terrorists, as shown in a poll a few weeks before the election by the University of Maryland's Program on International Policy Attitudes. The reframing worked.

• *Frames characterize ideas; they may be "deep" or "surface" frames.*
Deep frames structure your moral system or your worldview. Surface frames have a much smaller scope. They are associated with particular words or phrases, and with modes of communication. The reframing of the Iraq War as a "front in the war on terror" was a surface reframing. Words are defined mostly in terms of surface frames. Examples are labels like "death tax," "activist judges," "frivolous lawsuits," "liberal elites," and "politically correct," which are used by the right to trigger revulsion.

In politics, whoever frames the debate tends to win the debate. Over the past thirty-five years, conservatives have framed most of the issues in American political discourse.

• *Deep frames are where the action is.*
The deep frames are the ones that structure how you view the world. They characterize moral and political principles that are so deep they are part of your very identity. Deep framing is the conceptual infrastructure of the mind: the foundation, walls, and beams of that edifice. Without the deep frames, there is nothing for the surface message frames to hang on.

As we shall see, the conservative reframing of "freedom" is a deep reframing. The surface frames that go with slogans and clever phrases are effective only given the deep frames.

• *Most thought uses conceptual metaphors.*
Metaphorical thought is normal and used constantly, and we act on these metaphors. In a phrase like "tax relief," for example, taxation is seen as an affliction to be eliminated. Moral and political reasoning are highly metaphorical, but we are usually unaware of the metaphors we think with and live by.

• *Most thought does not follow the laws of logic.*
Thinking in frames and metaphors is normal and gives rise to inferences that do not fit laws of logic as mathematical logicians have formulated them. Political and economic reasoning uses frames and metaphors rather than pure laws of logic. Since metaphors and frames may vary from person to person, not all forms of reason are universal.

• *The frames and metaphors in our brains define common sense.*
Commonsense reasoning is just the reasoning we do using the frames and metaphors in our brains. The conservative domination of public political discourse has been changing what Americans mean by common sense.
 Our commonsense ideas may not fit the world. Frames and metaphors are mental constructs that we use to understand the world and to live our lives, but the world does not necessarily accommodate itself to our mental constructs.

• *Frames trump facts.*
Suppose a fact is inconsistent with the frames and metaphors in your brain that define common sense. Then the frame or metaphor will stay, and the fact will be ignored. For facts to make sense they must fit existing frames and metaphors in the brain.

Facts matter, and proper framing—both deep and surface—is needed to communicate the truth about our economic, social, and political realities.

Important national policies are made on the basis of deep frames, which characterize our most abiding values and define who we are morally, socially, and politically, and facts, that is, realities made urgent by those values. If facts are to make sense and be perceived as urgent, they must be framed in terms of the deep values that make them urgent.

- *Conservatives and progressives think with different frames and metaphors.*

In *Moral Politics*, I showed in great detail how complex conservative and progressive systems of thought are organized via metaphor around idealized models of strict father and nurturant parent families. This is hard to see when you think issue by issue, but it becomes clear when we understand how issues are organized across issue areas.

- *Contested concepts have uncontested cores.*

Important ideas like freedom that involve values and have a complex internal structure are usually contested—that is, different people have different understandings of what they mean. In general, contested concepts have uncontested cores—central meanings that almost everyone agrees on. The contested parts are left unspecified, blanks to be filled in by deep frames and metaphors.

For example, coercion impinges on freedom. But different people mean different things by "coercion." In the uncontested case, "coercion" is not further specified; it is left vague, a blank to be filled in.

- *Rational thought requires emotion.*

It used to be believed that emotion mostly interfered with rationality. But when people lose the capacity to feel emotions, they also lose the capacity to think rationally. Conservatives have learned far better than liberals how to take advantage of the links between emotion and rationality. They are especially adept at using fear to influence voters.

What does all this have to do with freedom? Everything.

As will become clear, freedom, like any other social and political concept, is composed of frames and metaphors. It is also what is called an "essentially contested concept": There will always be radical disagreement about it. It has an uncontested core that we all agree on. But it is a vague freedom; all the important blanks remain to be filled in. When the blanks are filled in by progressives and conservatives, what results are two radically different ideas expressed by the same word, "freedom." Currently, radical conservatives, as part of the "culture war" they have declared, are fighting to fill in the blanks and thereby redefine freedom in their way. Currently the right is winning this battle.

Americans need to know what is happening to their most precious idea.

A HIGHER RATIONALITY

I have two roles in this book. On the one hand, I am a linguist and a cognitive scientist. In this role, I am examining two very different forms of reason, in the service of a higher rationality that the tools of cognitive science provide. I believe it is vital to know how we think and to understand our forms of political discourse, to step outside of our own political beliefs and to see how moral and political reasoning work for both ourselves and others.

At stake here is the deepest form of freedom—the freedom that comes from knowing your own mind. If you are unaware of your own deep frames and metaphors, then you are unaware of the basis for your moral and political choices. Moreover, your deep frames and metaphors define the range within which your "free will" operates. You can't will something that is outside your capacity to imagine. Free will can operate only on ideas in your brain; it cannot operate on ideas you do not have.

Free will is thus not totally free. It is radically constrained by the frames and metaphors shaping your brain and limiting how you see the world. Those frames and metaphors get there, to a remarkable extent, through repetition in the media.

If this sounds a bit scary, it should. This is a scary time.

Cognitive science, by making us at least aware of alternative frames and metaphors, acts in the service of extending the range of free will.

Beyond writing as a scientist, I am also an advocate. I believe that one version of freedom is traditional and important to keep for the deepest moral reasons. I believe that the other version of freedom is dangerous to our democratic ideals and to the moral system behind the founding of our nation.

My task in this book is to open up a discussion of these two views of freedom, to describe them as accurately as possible, and to discuss how to take back the progressive view of freedom that lies at the heart of our democracy—and to do so honestly, using framings, both deep and surface, that we really believe and that reveal the truth about our social, economic, and political realities.

Traditional American freedom still reigns in the American mind. Nonetheless, the right has made serious inroads: Tens of millions of Americans now think about freedom through the right wing's framing of the idea, and the evidence of that is in elections, in polls, in legislation, in judicial decisions, and all around us on radio and TV. There is a real danger that the right will succeed. They have control of all branches of government.

They have a tight control on political infrastructure. They have the bully pulpit of the presidency. They have control of an important segment of the media (Fox and Clear Channel). And they have framed just about every issue in public debate so thoroughly and invisibly that even very intelligent, well-educated, savvy journalists don't notice. No, they haven't won, but they are making steady progress—and virtually without discussion.

The danger is not just a matter of words, a quibble over semantics. This is a war over an idea. If the idea of freedom changes radically, then freedom as we have known it is lost. The reason is that people act on their ideas. Ideas are not abstract things. They are components of action. They define ideals. They create norms of behavior. They characterize right and wrong, and accordingly change our understanding of the past and the present, our vision of the future, and even the laws of the land. Ownership of the word means ownership of the idea that goes with the word, and with it, domination of the culture defined by that idea.

Moreover, that domination does not end at our borders. The United States is the most powerful country on earth and it is dedicated to spreading its idea of freedom. Whose freedom will that be? If conservatives define foreign policy and control the definition of freedom itself, then the idea that they spread will not be the traditional American idea of freedom, but in many ways the very opposite.

The radical right knows the stakes. The culture war they have declared is real. All the outrages I listed above are real: the Iraq War and its death and destruction, the destruction of our environment, the shrinking of our civil liberties, the devastation of our economy, the weakening of our educational system—all real, too real.

THE PROGRESSIVES' MYSTERY

What progressives see as outrages conservative extremists hail as actions promoting freedom. Many progressives explain this by saying that conservatives are just greedy and mean. For the most part, I disagree. Some may be greedy and mean, but mostly they understand themselves as moral—but with a different morality.

Freedom, as they are redefining it, is the keystone at the base of this morality and its political agenda. It unifies radical conservative positions on issues across a wide spectrum of domestic and foreign policy. Progressives tend to fight issue by issue, while for the right, Bush's favorite phrase, "defending freedom" galvanizes the fight on many issues at once. Progressives are at a disadvantage against this worldview if they don't recognize it—and then counter it with a coherent and articulated vision of their own.

To illustrate this alien worldview, consider a line from George W. Bush's second inaugural address: "Self-government relies, in the end, on the government of the self." What does it mean? Why should it have a prominent place in his inaugural address?

I am not here to discuss mysteries for mystery's sake. If Americans are to hold on to freedom as they grew up with it, as they have come to know it and love it, then they have to understand that there is a radically different and frightening notion of what extremists on the right call "freedom" shaping our culture and our political life.

You can't stop it if you don't see it.

PART I

UNCONTESTED FREEDOM

1

FREEDOM IS FREEDOM IS FREEDOM

We all have what cognitive scientists call "folk theories," implicit understandings of how things work. How does a thermostat work? Or an electric lightbulb? Or color vision?

You might think that color is out there in the world and we just perceive it. That's a folk theory that virtually everyone has. In reality, there are no colors out there in the world. None! Objects reflect wavelengths, but wavelengths aren't colors. The experience of color is created by four factors: the wavelengths reflected by objects, the surrounding lighting conditions, the color cones in our eyes, and complex neural circuits in our brains. The activation of certain neurons is experienced as a given color. It may look to us like colors are out there in the things we see, but colors are really created through seeing with a body and brain.

For most people, it doesn't matter if their folk theory of color vision is false. They can go through life seeing colors, and even painting and mixing paints, perfectly well without ever knowing how color vision really works. But if you want to design a new color television or computer screen, you have to know more about how it really works.

We also have folk theories of language and thought. They too can be mistaken. For example, it is commonly thought that words have fixed meanings, and that their meanings are given by what they refer to in the world. The theory arises partly because of the way we learn words as children—parents say the word and point to, or hold up, the object. The theory—let's call it the single right meaning theory—says that there are clearly delineated sets of chairs and trees in the world, and "chair" refers to chairs, and "tree" refers to trees—and "freedom" refers to, well, freedom—a single, well-delineated condition in the world.

This is the common folk theory behind Elaine Kamarck's remark "Freedom is freedom is freedom," or Rush Limbaugh's refrain "Words mean things."

But in fact language is more complicated than that. "Over," for example, has *over* one hundred meanings, as, for example, in walk *over* the mountain, paint *over* the graffiti, *over*qualified, look it *over* but don't *over*look anything, and get *over* it! These happen to be systematically related in a complicated way but are still distinct.

"Freedom" is even more complicated. It is not a case where the word has many distinct meanings that we all agree on, like "over." The problem is not with the *word* but with the *idea*, the very concept of freedom. The idea of freedom has different interpretations, depending on your moral and political worldview.

But the folk theory of language, unlike the folk theory of color vision, has political consequences of the highest order! If most people think that the defining concept of this nation—freedom—has only one meaning, when it really has two almost opposite meanings, we are in an explosive situation, and one that can be manipulated by the side that is in power and has the most sway over the media, in this case, conservatives. It matters politically that the single right meaning folk theory is false.

A really obvious example where a given concept has multiple contested interpretations is art. Classical Western art is realist, depictive, and representational—art as imitation, paintings of landscapes and people, historical or mythical scenes, and everyday life. Modern art has challenged just about every precept of classical art, moving from realism to impressionism (the image is in the mind, not on the canvas), to abstraction (no depiction at all), to surrealism (depiction of the unreal), to abstract expressionism (expression of emotion), to field painting (exploration of color fields), to conceptual art (the art is in the idea), to performance art (the art is in what the artist does), and on and on.

Classical art is still the reference point from which other traditions diverge, and its traits define what is contested and changed. Those traits include form, color, an artist implementing an idea, a viewer's perception of the artwork. Think of the traits as blanks to be filled in, and the way they are filled in provides us with the various different understandings of what art is—realism, impressionism, surrealism, conceptual art. As we shall see, the concept of freedom works in a similar way: It too has an uncontested version and blanks to be filled in that produce different versions of freedom.

We owe a great deal to W. B. Gallie, a professor of political science at Cambridge University in England, who provided a deep insight into concepts like art and freedom in his classic essay, "Essentially Contested Concepts." Such concepts as freedom, democracy, and art are inherently subject to multiple interpretations, depending on your values, concerns, experiences, goals, and beliefs. Essentially contested concepts include such nonpolitical concepts as medicine (Western vs. Eastern; allopathic vs. homeopathic), economics (Keynesian vs. trickle-down), and even science itself (predictive, like classical physics, vs. explanatory, like evolution). Even the concept of a chair can be contested by competing schools of furniture design with different values, experiences, and goals. Can every concept be contested? We don't know for sure, but it would not be surprising.

This does not mean that concepts can be anything at all. Gallie's great contribution was to show that contested concepts arise in a systematic way. First, a contested concept has an uncontested core. The core concept picks out a well-known case or class of cases that is generally agreed on. Second, the concept must be evaluative, that is, it must be used to make value judgments. Third, it must have a complex structure—it must be complicated enough to allow for variations. And fourth, it has to have parts that are subject to variation; these are often underspecified, vague enough to allow details to be elaborated in more than one way.

Let's continue with the concept of art. Great classical art, say, a painting or sculpture by Michelangelo or another renowned artist, counts clearly as art—the uncontested core. Art can be good or bad in various ways, and it can be traditional or experimental, hence it is evaluative. A painting, for example, has a complex structure: its form, its colors, its role in art history, its social importance. This structure includes parts: the shapes, the colors, the idea to be implemented, how it is seen by a viewer, the artist's tools and techniques, its relationship to other artworks and to society. These parts provide choices among alternatives—the kinds of form, color, ideas, social issues, etc.— and opportunities for variation, and with them, opportunities for contestation. There are different ways to fill in the blanks in the complex concept. Are you painting a landscape, a person, or an abstraction? What kind of paints will you use? How will you apply the paint? Do you believe society is just? Should art reflect social conditions? Any reasonable level of complication can lead to contestation. It's normal.

FREEDOM

The radical right knows how to make political use of the uncontested cores of important concepts. In his second inaugural address, George W. Bush did not seem overtly to be using a definition of freedom fundamentally at odds with that of Democratic presidents. Indeed, the speech was careful not to be obvious about the difference. Bush makes it look as if he has the uncontested versions of traditional Democratic values: compassion, opportunity, life, and freedom. His radically different versions of those values go largely undiscussed in presidential discourse.

Bush contrasts freedom and liberty with slavery, oppression, tyranny, dictatorship, racism, and sexism. Indeed, the core concept of political freedom—the one we all share—includes frames that contrast with those frames. On the positive side, Bush identifies freedom with opportunity, justice, decency, tolerance, dignity, dissent, and participation. Superficially this may sound like the same idea of freedom put forth by Roosevelt, Kennedy, Johnson, and Martin Luther King.

But it is not.

To understand how and why, we must ask and answer a host of questions:

What, exactly, is the common uncontested core of the concept of freedom? Is it literal, and if not, what are its metaphors? What are its complexities? Why is it so easy for Bush to make it look like he shares traditional American values?

How does the common core get elaborated? Where are differences? How exactly, case by case, do the differences arise? What is their source? Are the differences random, or is there a systematic pattern?

SIMPLE FREEDOM

There is a simple understanding of freedom. Freedom is being able to do what you want to do, that is, being able to choose a goal, have access to that goal, pursue that goal without anyone purposely preventing you. It is having the capacity or power to achieve the goal and being able to exercise your free will to choose and achieve the goal.

Political freedom is about the state and how well a state can maximize freedom for all its citizens. A state can act to guarantee freedoms, to provide more freedom, or to take away freedom. From this perspective, states are to be judged on the basis of how well they guarantee freedoms for all their citizens and provide for as much freedom as possible, while restricting freedom as little as possible.

In America, democracy is usually seen as the form of government that maximizes freedom through its institutions: free elections, free press, civil liberties, free markets, civilian control of the military, freedom of religion, and checks and balances on the powers of the branches of government.

A free society is one in which such "basic freedoms" are guaranteed by the state.

That is the simple story, the story in which "freedom is freedom is freedom." If life were this simple, most Americans would agree that there is just one clear and uncontested idea of freedom.

But we don't all agree. Not even close. The disagreement is fostered first by the vagueness of simple freedom. All of the crucial parts of simple freedom are left unspecified. What is to count as free will, ability, and interference?

The disagreements get more complex as we move to political freedom. What exactly does it mean for a state to guarantee freedom, to provide more freedom or take freedoms away? When is an election free, what is a free press, what counts as civil liberties, what is a free market, when do civilians control the military, and how can checks and balances best be realized?

Every essential component of both simple freedom and political freedom is open to contestation. They are all blanks to be filled in with greater detail, and they are all subject to argument over the best way to fill in those blanks.

Given this situation, you might expect chaos, a concept of freedom so diverse as to be utterly confusing, with no two people ever agreeing. What is remarkable is that our different ideas about freedom are *not* completely chaotic. Instead, what we find are two radically different well-structured ideas, grounded in metaphors of the family, each with relatively minor variations that have vast implications. Freedom is complex, but manageably complex. In order to understand how these two different versions of freedom emerge, we first need to look more closely at the uncontested core they depend upon.

2

WHY FREEDOM IS VISCERAL

Much of everyday thought is metaphorical, and we scarcely notice it. We think of time in spatial terms with the future as ahead of us and the past as behind us. We "look forward" to an event in the future and "look back" at an event in the past. One event may be "farther in the past" than another event. The inference is that it happened first.

Even thought itself is commonly understood using metaphors. Knowing is metaphorically thought of in terms of seeing, as in, "Do you see what I mean?" This is not mere wordplay. It is a way of understanding what thought is in terms of what vision is. If my writing is "unclear," you won't know what I wrote. If a comment is "enlightening," it helps you understand. If a sentence is "opaque," you don't know what it means. Someone who kept you from knowing something can be said to have "pulled the wool over your eyes." Reasoning about knowing uses reasoning about seeing—via metaphorical thought. It is indeed "eye opening" to realize that our idea of something as apparently nonphysical as knowing is grounded firmly in the physical realm.

Metaphorical thought is tied to embodied experience—the experience of space in the first case above and the experience of vision in the second. Metaphorical thought links abstract ideas to visceral, bodily experiences.

FREEDOM

Freedom is a marvel of metaphorical thought. The idea of freedom is felt viscerally, in our bodies, because it is fundamentally understood in terms of our bodily experiences.

The language expressing the metaphorical ideas jumps out at you when you think of the opposite of freedom: "in chains," "imprisoned," "enslaved," "trapped," "oppressed," "held down," "held back," "threatened," "fearful," "powerless." We all had the experience as children of wanting to do something and being held down or held back, so that we were not free to do what we wanted. These bodily experiences form the basis of our everyday idea of simple freedom—for reasoning about freedom as well as for talking about freedom.

Freedom is being able to achieve purposes, either because nothing is stopping you or because you have the requisite capacities, or both. Much of what we seek to achieve is not just physical; our intended achievements normally extend to social realms: morality, politics, business, religion, communication, scholarship, art, and much more. Wherever there is an issue of setting and achieving goals, there is an issue of freedom—freedom thought of metaphorically, viscerally, in terms of functioning physically with your body in space to carry out some purposeful action.

Achieving purposes in general is understood metaphorically in three fundamental ways of functioning with one's body:

- Reaching a desired destination (by moving through space)
- Getting some desired object (by moving one's limbs)
- Performing a desired action (by moving one's body)

Thus, we think about achievements in terms of reaching goals (desired destinations), getting things you want (desired objects), and doing things (desired actions).

The metaphorical ideas are expressed in metaphorical language. If you are physically *in chains*, you can neither move through space nor move your limbs. You can't move where you want in space if you are *enslaved, imprisoned, trapped, held down,* or *held back.* You can't perform a desired action or get a desired object if you are *powerless, threatened by overwhelming force,* or *frozen with fear.* Why is there a program called Head Start? Because of the metaphor that life purposes are destinations to be reached. Freedom is the freedom to *go as far as you can* in life, to *get what you want* in life, or to *achieve what you can* in life.

Freedom requires access—to a location, to an object, or to the space to perform an action. Access is a crucial idea in human thought. It can mean physical access, as when the path is clear to move to a location or an object and you have the physical means to do so. Perceptual access, as when your gaze can "reach" an object or when sounds can reach your ears, is crucial for freedom. To reach a goal, you must first see it—or "see" it in your mind's eye. To heed a suspicion or respond to a calling, one must "hear"—literally or metaphorically.

You are not free to go somewhere, get something, or do something if access is blocked, or if there is no path (or road or bridge) to it. Freedom requires not just the *absence* of impediments to motion but also the *presence* of access. Inhibiting freedom is, metaphorically, not just throwing up roadblocks, holding one back, taking away power, imposing burdens or threats or harm, but also failing to provide access. Freedom may thus require creating access, which may involve building.

The metaphor of freedom as freedom of motion thus has two important parts: freedom *from* and freedom *to.* Freedom from concerns those things that can keep you from moving. Freedom to concerns making sure there is access. Thus you might be mentally or psychologically *blocked,* emotionally *powerless* or *threatened,* or lack the *access* that education and knowledge provide for achievement.

We can now see why freedom is a visceral concept. It is tied, fundamentally via metaphor, to our ability to move and to interference with moving. There is little that is more infuriating than interference with our everyday bodily movements. It is the embodiment of freedom via metaphor that makes it such an important and emotionally powerful concept.

FREEDOM AND THE PURPOSEFUL LIFE

Part of being an American, culturally, goes beyond achieving isolated purposes to having a purposeful life. Thus, life itself becomes structured in terms of space—goals you want to reach (where you want to be in life), things you want to get (rewards, awards, things that symbolize success), and things you want to do or achieve. Dreams are seen as lifetime purposes. "The American Dream" is based on this metaphor. Freedom then becomes being free to *live the dream*, with nothing holding you back or keeping you down.

Another important American metaphor is based on the idea of essences—essential properties (or capacities or abilities) that each person has within himself or herself. To live a purposeful life is to discover that essence and actualize it. Freedom here is freedom to *be all that you can be*, with nothing preventing us from realizing the potential to transform ourselves according to that essence.

These metaphors can be applied to any area of life: economic, social, aesthetic, political, religious, academic. For example, suppose you love art, have artistic talent, and decide you want to pursue a career as a visual artist. What does it mean to be free to do so? You will need access to an art school to develop your talent. That means a school will have to have a place for you, you will have to be admitted, you will have to have the money to attend, you will need to be sufficiently free of personal obligations, you will have to have the fortitude to go through rigorous training, and you will have to be able to exercise your free will every step of the way without internal hang-ups stopping you. In short, the freedoms required to pursue a particular purposeful life may be extensive.

That such freedoms are needed is uncontested. What may be contested is how these freedoms are defined. Are they personal or political freedoms? Views differ, depending on what one takes to be the role of the state. For example, a state may shut down art schools in a crackdown on art as degenerate. That seems clearly an issue of political freedom. But suppose a government decided simply to defund public art programs, thinking art to be frivolous or unfriendly to its political agenda. Is that an imposition on political freedom? This would seem to be contestable, as are other cases: Political decisions about the economy may produce a depression, making it impossible for one to have the money to attend. A major hurricane may wipe out your hometown and destroy your home, or destroy the art school, because of political decisions about the priorities to be given to disaster relief. One may be a single parent of modest means requiring child care, and the state may not provide child care for single parents seeking an education. In short, the line between personal and political freedom is contestable in a wide range of cases.

The idea of a purposeful life makes freedom of central importance. Freedom—of many kinds—is required if you are to achieve your purposes in life. If you have goals, needs, or dreams, or require fulfillment in life—and Americans are supposed to have all of these—then the freedoms to achieve them become of uppermost importance, and the contestation over which of these are personal and which political is a serious issue.

Moreover, if you are a fundamentalist Christian and believe in "the purpose-driven life," where God has a purpose for you and you have to achieve it to get into heaven and avoid the eternal torture of hell, the freedoms required to achieve God's purpose for you take on cosmic proportions.

FREEDOM OF THE WILL

At the heart of any social, moral, or political notion of freedom is freedom of the will. This is another case where metaphorical thought is busy at work.

We all do some things and not other things. Many are in our conscious control, and many are not. We cannot consciously control the beating of our hearts, the digestion of food, the feeling of pain, what sounds sound like to us, and so on. The same is true of what we think. Most thought is unconscious; as cognitive science has found, conscious thought is the tip of the iceberg of all the thinking we do. Yet we can consciously give in to a desire, make a plan, or set a priority—and we can consciously make a decision based on our evaluation of the pros and cons of our possible actions.

In the Western tradition, we have metaphorically understood this kind of decision making as if it were executed by a person-like entity residing in our minds whose job is to choose how we act—the "will." In the Enlightenment, there was an elaborate metaphorical folk theory, called faculty psychology, in which the mind was a kind of society, with members who were individuals with different jobs. Among the members of the society of mind were Perception, Reason, Passion, Judgment, and Will. Perception gathered the sense data from the outside world; Reason figured out the consequences; Passion was the locus of desire; Will controlled action; and when Passion and Reason were in a standoff as to what Will should do, Judgment made the decision. Decision making was seen as a tug-of-war between Reason, who informs, and Passion, who just pulls us off the track. Will can be strong or weak. To stand up to the pull of Passion, Will has to be strong. If Will acts according to the dictates of Reason, Will makes rational decisions. If Will is weak, it gives in to the tug of Passion and acts irrationally. And where there is a standoff, good Judgment is necessary for rational, sensible action. If this makes sense to you, you are still living with this seventeenth-century metaphor—as most Americans seem to be.

One of our most common metaphors for thought is motion in space, where the mind moves through space, where ideas are locations, and where reason is a force that pushes the mind in certain directions. If we are rational, we think *step-by-step* and directly, not *in circles*. If we don't pay attention, our thoughts may *wander*. But if we think according to the force of reason, we will reach a rational conclusion.

When these two metaphors are combined, we get the idea of freedom of the will. Will is free to move in any direction, free to follow the course of reason or the pull of passion. But a person who is free, rational, and responsible uses free will as constrained by reason and good judgment. Thus, freedom in the simple case is not irrational free action or irresponsible free action left to wander willy-nilly. It is action that follows a particular path toward specific goals. The battle between reason and passion is the background to the very idea of discipline—directing the motion of our will according to reason.

Free will, understood in this way, is central to simple freedom, which is viscerally grounded in the freedom to move. Both freedom from and freedom to have their metaphorical sources in motion toward a goal. It is free will that chooses that goal. And it is free will, following the dictates of reason and judgment, that chooses rational and reasonable goals. And since a purposeful life is commonly conceptualized as a lengthy journey on which many decisions as to direction must be made, free will is used over and over.

The will is internal; what keeps it from operating freely is also

understood as internal—usually as some form of passion or emotion. Thus we speak of "emotional blockages," irrational forces
that constrain the will.

Another impediment to freedom of the will is metaphorical
slavery, being a slave to drugs, to sex, to religion, to one's job, to
peer pressure, to money or fame—to anything that rules over the
exercise of one's free will, rationality, and good judgment. The
slavery metaphor characterizes a systematic weakness of the will
with respect to a given factor. In the metaphor, the will is enslaved and too weak to overpower the master, and so has no
choice but to do what is commanded by some kind of passion:
sexual desire, greed, a need for peer acceptance, religious fervor,
or duty.

One's will may also be overwhelmed momentarily or occasionally, say by sexual desire or peer pressure or drugs—as if
engulfed by an unexpected wave of irresistible force. Both
metaphors characterize real experiences, but there is a difference
in social acceptability. It is usually seen as normal to be occasionally overwhelmed by unpredictable experiences seen as exerting
real force over one's normal behavior. But it is less socially ac-
ceptable to be "enslaved" by any experience, since it is predictable. It is assumed that, if an experience of weakness of the
will is predictable, one can develop the strength of will to free
oneself. Nancy Reagan's "Just say no" campaign was a denial of
both metaphors with respect to drugs. It was assumed that one's
will was always strong enough to resist.

What keeps an individual from acting freely in the simple
everyday situations?

- Internal impediments: emotional blockages, slavery to
  passions, or being overwhelmed, that is, a will weak in
  the face of some emotion or passion
- External impediments: an external authority, an enemy, or a lack of access (a lack of ability or resources)

These are all cases in which your exercise of free will cannot govern your actions, for one reason or another. Thus, freedom, in simple everyday cases, consists in the ability of free will to govern one's actions—in accordance with the force of reason and good judgment, and free from both internal and external impediments.

A political metaphor used to characterize the internal aspect of freedom is that of self-rule or self-government: having a will that is able to overcome emotions and passions and act freely, to govern one's own choices and actions. That is, freedom requires free will: government of the self by the self. Since the goals of a free person are set according to free will, they are goals for oneself. Thus, freedom requires government of the self, by the self, and for the self. In short, there is a metaphorical parallel between freedom for an individual and freedom in a democracy.

We can see such a parallel as well in the metaphor of the body politick, which has played an important role in our political tradition. The idea of the society of mind may seem anachronistic today for talking about a person, but it has had important historical effects. In the body politick metaphor, the society of mind maps onto politics roughly as follows: Reason is the legislature (which makes the laws), will is the administration (which executes the laws), and judgment is the judiciary (which resolves disputes). A rational, well-functioning society is one that follows the rule of law, where will acts in accord with reason and good judgment—just as a rational, well-functioning person would.

This metaphor is the rationale for the infrastructure of a democratic government in a free society. It involves more than just a separation and balance of powers to prevent the tyranny of the will, that is, the administration that executes the laws. It is also a definition and separation of functions required for a rational, well-functioning free society. When new democracies are formed on the model of older democracies, this is the structure that it seems natural to impose.

Thus the idea of simple freedom for a person in everyday situations translates into simple political freedom via a set of common metaphors.

Simple freedom, as we are characterizing it, is the uncontested version of freedom shared by both conservatives and progressives. It leaves blanks—ideas that are unspecified and that distinguish progressives from conservatives. One of those blanks is the nature of the capacity for self-government, both in the individual and in society. Does it come about by domination (strength of the will) or by a cooperative balance of powers (of reason, will, passion, and judgment)?

Interestingly enough, even with all the blanks left unspecified, there is a logic of simple freedom, which is the subject of the next chapter.

It is important to recognize that uncontested simple freedom does not include certain historical forms of contested freedom. The idea that free will should be constrained by what we normally mean by rationality and good judgment has been repeatedly contested. Versions of freedom exist that are overtly antirational (surrealism and dadaism in art) or that see freedom, not slavery, in the use of drugs ("Tune in, turn on, drop out") and unconstrained sexuality (sexual liberation and libertinism), or in "slavishly" following religious dogma. On the left, these are commonly part of one form of counterculture politics (anarchism) or certain art movements. On the right, they are typically forms of radical laissez-faire capitalism, extreme militarism, fascism, or radical fundamentalism based on pure faith and revelation. All of these cases are real—and important to bear in mind. Both the right and the left like to parody each other in terms of the other's real, but extreme, antirational movements.

Such movements are outside of both the progressive and conservative norms that we will be discussing. It is common for progressives and conservatives to label each other in terms of such extreme cases. So far, the right has been more effective, labeling liberals falsely as "doing what feels good" and advocating a breakdown of morality, or as potheads and airheads. The far left has been less effective in characterizing conservatives as fascists.

Simple freedom at its most visceral is physical and nonmetaphorical. It is freedom to move to achieve physical purposes (either reaching a destination, getting an object, or performing an action). But simple freedom is extended metaphorically to achieving any kind of purpose—typically in a social realm, including morality, politics, business, art. A further metaphor—the society of mind metaphor—projects freedom onto the will, properly governed by reason and judgment, but pulled in a destructive way by passion.

Understanding simple freedom in this way happens to remove classical philosophical puzzles. For example, if freedom involves satisfying desires (or achieving purposes), is freedom increased if desire is removed? No. Freedom makes sense only in the frame of achieving purposes (satisfying desires). If the frame ceases to be applicable, freedom, which is defined only relative to that frame, makes little if any sense.

Or take another puzzle: Suppose I desire to be a slave. Do I become free if my desire is fulfilled? No. The frame in which freedom is defined requires access and lack of impediments. Once you become a slave, the frame, when applied, says you are not free.

The point of these examples is that freedom is a frame-based concept, defined within a mental structure and not just free-floating. And even in its simple uncontested form, it is thoroughly metaphorical, which means that, though it is abstract, it is grounded viscerally in bodily experience. The apparent paradoxes above emerge from a false theory of mind and language that assumes that freedom can be defined abstractly on its own terms, frame free and metaphor free.

3

THE LOGIC OF SIMPLE FREEDOM

Freedom is not a simple matter. The progressive and conservative versions are radically different. But they do share a core idea and a core logic, which we are calling simple freedom.

Characterizing the uncontested version of the most central—yet the most contested—concept in our national life is an achievement. Avoiding contestation often means leaving details vague and unspecified and avoiding the hard cases. Thus, the logic of simple, uncontested freedom will not cover all the cases—only the uncomplicated cases.

For example, the idea of simple freedom involves the idea of harm, as in freedom from harm. But harm itself is a contested concept; it means very different things to progressives and conservatives. The logic of simple freedom also involves ideas like nature and competition. These ideas too are contested and mean very different things to progressives and conservatives. But as long as one sticks to the uncontested cores of these concepts, a logic exists.

I'll be discussing that logic in this chapter, which is divided into three parts:

- First, the logic of imposing on someone's freedom. This will include a discussion of harm, coercion, security, property, rights, justice, order and rule of law, fairness, and equality.

- Second, the situations where freedom does not arise as an issue, that is, where an interference with someone's achieving his or her purposes is not normally seen as an infringement on freedom. We will discuss the important cases of competition and nature.

- Third, there is political freedom. Here we will discuss how freedom enters into just about all of our basic political ideas: fairness, equality, opportunity, self-government, and so on.

Harm, coercion, nature, competition, fairness, equality, and all the others are, in the versions discussed in this chapter, simple uncontested versions of contested concepts. They are vague components of the concept of simple freedom—blanks to be fleshed out in contested cases. Discussing how they can be fleshed out will make it strikingly clear why freedom is a contested idea and how two different versions of this idea have emerged in our polarized nation.

IMPOSING ON FREEDOM

The most basic assumption of simple freedom is that *being free does not make you free to interfere with the freedom of others.*

This is clear in the simple cases. You are walking down the street. Others are not free to step in front of you and stop you. Except of course if they are serving the greater cause of freedom (for others) by doing so, for example, if you are a fugitive from justice and the police stop you and take you in.

Other cases are equally obvious. Your freedom does not make you free to enslave other people, or to grab them and tie them up, or to keep them from earning a living, or to keep them from speaking freely or freely associating with others.

The contestation arises over what counts as interference and whether other factors override the no-interference condition. For example, are you free to burn a fire in your fireplace if the smoke badly pollutes the neighborhood and makes it hard for your neighbors to breathe? That is highly contested in many places in America. Are you free to jump right in front of someone walking down the street and throw him off balance and make him fall? Usually not, but if you are trying to keep a child from running into a busy street and being hit by a car, then yes. Overriding factors do exist.

HARM

• *Harm (sufficient to interfere with normal functioning) is interference with freedom.*
If someone breaks your leg, she is interfering with your freedom to move. If someone kills you, he is interfering with your freedom to live your life.

The matter is trickier with metaphorical harm. There is, for example, economic harm. Suppose someone steals your money or your property and it interferes with your normal functioning (spending your money or using your property). You may not be physically hurt, but we typically count this as harm.

Then there are other forms of metaphorical harm—psychological or emotional harm, for example. Or harm to one's reputation. If severe enough, they may count as interfering with your freedom as well.

Again there is a question of what counts as harm. Many conservatives believe that social programs harm people because they make them dependent on the government, while progressives tend to believe that they help people. Many progressives believe that a low minimum wage harms workers, while conservatives tend to believe that raising the minimum wage would harm business.

COERCION

One of our major metaphors for the freedom to engage in purposeful action is the freedom to move to a desired destination. Purposes are understood as goals, as places you're trying to get to. It's harder when someone stands in your way, or holds you down, or holds you back, or forces you to go somewhere you don't want to go. When someone purposefully does any of those things, he or she is interfering with your freedom of motion. An important case is coercion. Coerced action is, metaphorically, forced motion to an undesired location.

- *Coercion interferes with freedom.*

Coercion is a major theme in discussions of freedom, and it comes in many forms. Further metaphors map physical coercion onto economic coercion, social coercion, and religious coercion. In short, forms of coercion occur in any domain where there are goals and forces that can interfere with them.

What counts as coercion is contested. If an atheist child is forced to say the Pledge of Allegiance containing "under God" or forced to listen to Christian school prayers, is that coercion? Even if there is no physical force, but "merely" peer pressure? Is a teacher in a public school subject to coercion if she can't discuss intelligent design?

PROPERTY

Another common metaphor for the idea of achieving a purpose is the idea of getting a desired object. According to this metaphor, the freedom to achieve one's purposes is, metaphorically, the lack of any interference in getting and keeping desired objects.

This fundamental metaphor thus creates a conceptual link between freedom and property: Freedom is, in this metaphor, the freedom to acquire and keep property. Moreover, the property itself can be metaphorical, such as intellectual property.

But there is also a literal link between freedom and property. Considerable wealth can buy many kinds of freedom—the freedom to travel and live where one wants, to acquire objects, to have protection (guards, gated communities), to do things the less wealthy cannot afford to do. Both literally and metaphorically,

- *Property means freedom.*

But it is often contested whether certain property is properly yours. Take the issue of taxes. Conservatives say, "It's your money. The government wants to take it away." But almost everyone gains part of his or her income through the use of a government-supplied infrastructure (highways, the Internet, the banking system, the courts). Is there a moral debt to pay to maintain that system? If there is, then not all of your income is "your money." You may have it in hand, but you owe some to your country. "Your money" is your income minus that debt, that is, minus taxes. Needless to say, this is a contested idea.

SECURITY

If harm, coercion, and limitations on property interfere with freedom, then security is a guarantee that such freedom will be preserved. Just as physical harm and physical coercion are the prototypical forms of harm and coercion—what we first think when we think of harm and coercion—so physical security is the prototypical form of security. Physical security of oneself and one's property is central to the concept of freedom.

And just as harm and coercion come in many forms—economic, social, psychological—so security does as well. If economic harm is a loss of money or property sufficient to affect normal functioning, so economic security is a protection from economic harm.

• *Security guarantees freedom from harm.*
What is contested here is: Who is responsible for guaranteeing which forms of freedom, the individual or the state? With Social Security, there is a government guarantee of at least some freedom from economic harm in old age. Conservatives say that the moral obligation to guarantee freedom from economic harm in old age rests with the individual, not the government.

RIGHTS

Rights are understood via a small complex of metaphors. First, they are metaphorical possessions, things you can have and that people can try to take away. Rights are a metaphorical form of property.

Second, rights are like metaphorical tickets to a certain kind of freedom; a right grants you free passage to a desired situation, that is, a situation in which you can engage in a desired course of action (a right to speak your mind) or receive some benefit (a right to unemployment insurance).

There are kinds of rights; for example, moral rights, legal rights, and political rights. Rights are specific to particular domains: morality, law, and politics. A moral right may not be a legal right or a political right.

Some rights are quite simple-minded. Suppose you buy a ticket to a movie. That ticket gives you the right to a seat for the duration of the film.

In law, real property (real estate) is understood as a bundle of rights, rights of use, access, extraction, and transfer. Each of these confers a different kind of benefit. Since the rights that constitute property are themselves understood as kinds of property, it is not surprising that such rights can be bought and sold.

Other rights cannot be bought, sold, or transferred. Laws specify which rights function in which way. For example, a couple may give a child up for adoption, that is, they may transfer to others the right to raise their child. Other rights are not transferable, such as spousal rights, the right to file a joint tax return, the right to community property, or the right to receive pension benefits upon the death of a spouse. Rights may be property, but there are laws governing the transfer of property.

Because rights are conceptualized as property, and since taking away property is conceptualized as a form of harm, taking away a right is conceptualized as an imposition on freedom.

- *Taking away a right is imposing on freedom.*
- *Guaranteeing a right is guaranteeing a freedom.*

What is contested here is whether a given right exists, or should exist. For example, does a homosexual couple in a stable and loving relationship have a right to marry? Should they be *free* to marry? Should a farmer whose farm is in a no-sprawl zone that prevents housing developments have the right to sell his farm to a developer? Should he be *free* to dispose of his property in any way at all that he chooses?

HUMAN RIGHTS

The link between freedom and human nature brings up the question of inalienable rights—human rights, rights that we have simply via our human nature and that cannot be given up or taken away, since we are and remain human beings. The Bill of Rights specifies those rights that cannot be taken away by a government. They are specified in terms of freedoms: freedom of speech, association, religion, and so on.

There is a general principle behind inalienable human rights:

• *Human rights confer the freedom to do what is natural and normal for any human being.*
It's natural to eat and drink and sleep and to sit down when you're tired. When African Americans were denied access to Woolworth lunch counters, to water fountains, and to hotels, they were being denied their inalienable rights. When Rosa Parks sat down on that bus, she asserted a human right.

If guaranteeing a right is guaranteeing a freedom—either a freedom from harm or coercion or a freedom to achieve some desired state—then someone must be responsible for guaranteeing that right. For every right, there is a responsibility. The freedoms that come from rights are meaningless in the absence of people carrying out those responsibilities.

In certain cases of legal rights, governments hire and pay people to carry out the responsibility of guaranteeing rights, the police and the courts. But, for the most part,

• *A free society requires that its citizens, as a matter of civic duty, be responsible for helping to guarantee the rights of others, as well as our own rights.*
In short, rights are possessions that you acquire, and there is a debt to pay: civic duty, the responsibility to see that the rights of others are guaranteed.

Rights cannot be taken for granted. If not exercised, rights—the rights of all—may cease to exist. It is thus a civic responsibility to exercise one's rights.

Responsibilities are often contested. If the indigent have a right to food so they don't starve to death, who has the responsibility to feed them? Is it the state, through supplying food stamps paid for by taxes? Progressives see feeding the poor as a responsibility required of the citizenry. Some conservatives argue that using tax money forces the responsibility on the public and that the responsibility should be freely undertaken, say, by private charities or churches. They see this as a matter of freedom—freedom from the forced imposition of a responsibility for someone else.

JUSTICE

Justice is commonly understood in terms of moral accounting, a metaphorical system in which well-being is understood as a form of wealth, and harm as a taking of wealth. Justice, in this metaphor, is a balancing of the moral books—either punishment of the wrongdoer (paying one's debt to society) or compensation of the victim by the wrongdoer (paying in recompense for the harm done). The books may be balanced in various ways: retribution—harm to the victim is balanced by harm to the perpetrator; and restitution—harm to the victim is balanced by a contribution to society, say, being sentenced to clean up the freeway or work in an AIDS hospice.

Imprisonment—taking away freedom—is a metaphorical (as well as a quite real) form of harm. Punishment by imprisonment for harm (physical or economic) is the metaphorical balancing of harm with harm, retributive justice.

The civil justice system uses lawsuits to punish a corporation for harming people (retribution) by forcing it to pay the victims (restitution). Under the metaphor of well-being as wealth, monetary compensation for harm (taking away well-being) is restoring the balance by giving real wealth to counter the loss of metaphorical wealth (well-being).

What does justice have to do with freedom? They are intimately intertwined by the following logic.

In punishing those who do harm (physical harm, economic

harm, or interference with one's rights), we take justice to be a necessary deterrent that promotes freedom from harm, threat, and fear. In addition, through imprisonment (the taking of freedom), it can remove from society, at least for a time, those who have taken freedom from others both literally (through assault, rape, and murder) as well as metaphorically, that is, those who have caused harm, imposed coercion, or taken property.

Thus,

- *Justice is required for freedom in a free society.*
- *Injustice is therefore an imposition on freedom.*

Injustice—the failure to punish or compensate, or the punishment of the wrong person—leaves those who impose on the freedom of others free to continue to harm the innocent directly and contributes to a failure of deterrence, which contributes indirectly to the harm of those who are innocent. That is what makes injustice an imposition on freedom.

The converse is true as well.

- *Freedom is required for justice.*

In a society run by tyranny or corruption, justice can be denied by the will of the tyrant or through corruption. For a system of justice to work, a minimal condition is freedom from tyranny and corruption. In our system of justice, the jury that decides the case must be able to exercise free will, tempered by reason and good judgment, which are to be checked by the other jurors. Moreover, a defendant must be able to be free to put up the best defense possible. Justice is denied if the jury is intimidated (and cannot exercise free will) or if the defendant is denied the opportunity to (that is, is not free to) put up his or her best defense.

Where is the contestation?

Progressives argue that, in many cases, justice—taken to be a strict eye-for-an-eye balancing of the moral books—is not required for freedom. Take the death penalty. It does not deter murders, and so it does not contribute to freedom from harm. On the contrary, it violates human rights. It increases the amount of harm done in the world without preventing any. And it makes the state an agent of murder—an agent of ultimate harm toward its own citizens.

Conservatives counter that, without such punishment, our entire system of morality would break down. Without the death penalty, the books cannot be properly balanced. Moreover, the families of murder victims have suffered a loss. They often feel that their loss should be balanced by the loss of the murderer's life.

Conservatives argue against the United States submitting to the jurisdiction of the World Court, which would probably convict some high U.S. officials as war criminals. Conservatives argue that, in giving up any sovereignty at all to a world body, the United States would be surrendering its freedom. Progressives counter that war criminals *should* be brought to justice no matter who they are, and especially if they are high U.S. officials, thus protecting people from harm and enhancing their freedom.

THE RULE OF LAW

The rule of law has two aspects: the laws and their enforcement. Laws are guidelines for action.

• *Ideally, laws function in the service of freedom, attempting to guarantee that there will be no serious harm, no undue coercion, and no taking of—or restricted access to—property.*

Enforcement is the use of force to guarantee that the laws will be followed. This use of coercion is seen as functioning positively in the service of freedom.

This idea was most famously expressed by Rousseau in his metaphor of the social contract—the exchange of absolute freedom and its dangers, which threaten freedom, for freedom within a social order maintained by force, where most of the threat to an individual's freedom from another's violence is removed. Absolute freedom is exchanged for security, which guarantees other freedoms. Security yields order. Order is necessary for freedom.

- *A threat to order is a threat to freedom.*

Progressives have long contested the absolute version of this principle, arguing that civil disobedience is often necessary for freedom, especially when the guardians of order are themselves unjust. But civil disobedience, which is usually limited and nonviolent, is conducted not to overthrow order and the rule of law, but rather to make them more just. Progressive protests of all sorts use civil disobedience, demonstrating for civil rights, workers' rights, women's rights, immigrant rights, gay rights, and so on. Recently, conservatives have discovered civil disobedience, with demonstrations for the "right to life" in cases of abortion, stem cell research, and euthanasia.

EQUALITY AND FAIRNESS

Freedom, equality, and fairness are linked, in the uncontested cases, by a tight logic. Rules by a dictator create inequality and unfairness. Only freedom—understood as self-government—permits equality and fairness. It is equality under the law that justifies the rule of law in a democracy. Justice—a balancing of the moral books—is seen as fairness and hence as equal treatment.

Fairness is, however, highly contested, as is equality. Here are some examples of what is considered fair:

- Equality of distribution (one child, one cookie)
- Equality of opportunity (one person, one raffle ticket)

- Procedural distribution (playing by the rules determines what you get)
- Equal distribution of power (one person, one vote)
- Equal distribution of responsibility (we share the burden equally)
- Scalar distribution of responsibility (the greater your abilities, the greater your responsibilities)
- Scalar distribution of rewards (the more you work, the more you get)
- Rights-based fairness (you get what you have a right to)
- Need-based fairness (you get what you need)
- Contractual distribution (you get what you agree to)

Here one can see clearly some of the ways that fairness and equality are contested. For example, where progressives tend to support equality of distribution and need-based fairness, conservatives prefer equality of opportunity and contractual fairness.

We have been tracing the logic of freedom by looking at where one person imposes on the freedom of another: harm, coercion, the taking of property, the taking of rights, and injustice. Correspondingly, security, justice, the rule of law, fairness, and equality contribute to the idea of freedom.

In all the cases of imposition on freedom, it is a person who interferes with another's freedom. And in all cases, there is a possibility of *not* imposing, of not interfering with someone else achieving his or her goals. When corporations are metaphorically thought of as persons, then the courts can see corporations as interfering with the freedoms of their customers, their employees, or the public.

If these two conditions hold in all cases of the imposition on freedom, what happens in cases where one or the other does *not* hold? In those cases there can be no imposition on freedom.

That is, the issue of freedom, or of the imposition on it, cannot arise. In short, these two conditions define the limits of the application of the idea of freedom.

WHERE FREEDOM CANNOT BE ABRIDGED

If a storm were to cut your telephone lines, it would be odd to think of that as an abridgment of your freedom. But if the FBI were to cut your telephone lines, it would definitely be an abridgment of your freedom.

Suppose the Texas Rangers baseball team is playing the Oakland As in the playoffs. If the Rangers win fair and square, it would not be considered an abridgment of Oakland's freedom. But if the president ordered the As to be arrested and held as suspected terrorists just until they forfeited the playoff games to Texas, that would be an abridgment of their freedom.

Why?

In all cases of interference with freedom, someone's purposes are thwarted. The converse is not true. Purposes can be thwarted without it being an issue of freedom. Under what circumstances is this true?

The most interesting cases I have found are those of natural causes and competition. What makes these cases interesting is that the concepts of nature and competition are both contested, and the issue of whether or not freedom has been abridged depends on how they are contested.

NATURE

The laws of the natural world constrain us. I am not free to float up off the ground or to dematerialize here and materialize in

Paris. Yet this does not count as an interference with my freedom. What defies physical possibility is not seen as an abridgment of freedom. There is no disagreement here.

What is physically impossible for all human beings doesn't count. Our physical nature is taken for granted. Freedom is about possibility, and how other people interfere with it. Where there is no possibility, there can be no interference.

Nature can impose harm, exert overpowering force, take your property, and make it impossible to do what normal human beings do. And nature is certainly not just! But an earthquake is not seen as an abridgment of freedom, though a terrorist attack is. The difference is whether the imposition has a human or natural cause.

Human nature, as we have seen, matters in a different way for freedom. When nature is internal to a human being, the human being has no possibility but to act according to his or her nature. Being born left-handed is not seen as an abridgment of your freedom. Nor is being born short.

What we take to be human nature is central to the American idea of freedom. In general, we are free to engage in behavior that is understood as natural and normal. Within the uncontested range, freedom extends to engaging in trade (but not selling secrets), expressing your ideas (but not identifying an undercover CIA agent), associating with people of one's choice (except in the case of conspiracy). These are called inalienable rights—freedom of speech, assembly, association, and so on.

But what counts as "natural and normal" is often contested. Conservatives, for example, talk constantly about the "homosexual lifestyle"—a frame that takes homosexuality out of the arena of nature and into the arena of human choice. Progressives, correspondingly, argue that homosexuality is a matter of nature, not "lifestyle," and is therefore a matter of inalienable rights. Marriage for homosexuals is seen as a freedom issue.

COMPETITION

Consider cases of scarce resources, where there is not enough for everyone. These are situations defined by the fact that not everyone can achieve his or her goals. When one person gets a scarce resource, another person may be automatically precluded from getting it. There is no possibility for everyone to freely get the scarce resource.

Such cases often explicitly or implicitly fall under the category of competition. Freedom to compete is a form of freedom.

But what happens when you are in a competition? Is winning a competition interfering with the freedom of the losers? The answer is no. The category of a competition removes the issue of interfering with the freedom of the others in the competition. When Tiger Woods wins a golf tournament, he is not abridging the freedom of the other players. One company is not seen as interfering with the freedom of another if it makes a better product that the public buys and thereby puts the other company out of business.

However, it is common for there to be rules and laws governing competition. If the rules or laws are violated, the result may be injustice, and injustice does impose on freedom. Thus, in the competition for jobs, unjust hiring practices can be abridgments of freedom.

There are also mores governing competitions. When Wal-Mart enters a small community, it often puts small local shops out of business, paying lower wages and offering no medical benefits, often forcing the community to pay for emergency medical care. Progressives tend to see this not as fair competition but as an unethical "raid" on a community—and an imposition on its freedom.

The contestation here is a question of what is to count as competition and how the rules that govern the competition are defined. Take the question of college admissions and affirmative action. In the case of Proposition 209 in California some years ago, conservatives framed college admissions in terms of a competition for admission. In the American tradition of fairness in competition, the criteria should be clear and objective—say, grades and SAT scores—and race, gender, and ethnicity should be irrelevant.

But the university did not consider admissions exclusively in terms of a competition over grades and standardized test scores. It saw the real competition outside the university—in the job market and in impoverished communities' need for skilled professionals. The university saw admissions as part of a complex moral mission: not just to educate the best and the brightest, those with the highest GPAs and test scores, but also to provide social, cultural, and educational capital to minority students who were talented but who historically lacked access to this capital. The university's goal was to give minorities a fair chance in the job market and to train professionals—doctors, teachers, lawyers, and engineers—who wanted to work in underserved communities. These are freedom issues, not in admissions but in the world outside the university, and the university saw itself as promoting freedom, as providing access, in the world at large. The university also saw its educational mission as providing a culturally diverse student body, which would promote tolerance (freedom from discrimination) and help to educate students about California's diverse cultural heritage (freedom of access to knowledge).

The university failed in communicating its moral and educational mission to the public, while conservative opponents succeeded in framing admissions purely as a competition to be conducted fairly according to a narrow body of criteria, where unfair competition (based on race and ethnicity) compromised freedom.

Another example of contestation over what counts as competition is the issue of whether "intelligent design" is to be taught as science. Advocates of intelligent design have based

their public relations campaign on the two very different meanings of the word "theory." In everyday speech, there is a frame
concerning truth. A "theory" is not an established truth and
contrasts with a "fact." "Just a theory" in this frame suggests that
there is no good reason to believe it.

But science is about more than mere belief or conjecture. Science is fundamentally a moral enterprise, following the moral
imperative to seek the truth. Science is fundamentally about
freedom, freedom of inquiry into the truth without the bias of
initial faith or belief. Within science as an institution, a "scientific theory" is in fact a material explanation of a huge range of
data based on experiment and evidence. Within science, it is
normal for theories to compete. The basis of competition is
clear: amount of evidence, convergence of independent evidence from many areas, coverage of data, crucial experiments,
degree and depth of explanation. The judges of the competition
are distinguished scientists who have spent their careers studying
the scientific evidence.

In the science of biology, evolution wins the competition,
governed by the rules of the scientific method, hands down.
There are no other legitimate competitors. Freedom here is freedom of objective inquiry, on the basis of evidence and explanation. Other theories are free to enter the competition, but if
they do not follow the rules of the competition, they will be
eliminated—fairly and justly.

Intelligent design advocates, who are often fundamentalist
Christians, argue that living creatures are too well and intricately
"designed" to have evolved without a designer—namely, God.
Advocates of intelligent design refuse to accept the rules governing the competition. They frame science merely as belief. Their
"theory" is as good as anybody else's. In matters of belief, there
should be no prejudice. Freedom here is freedom of expression,
freedom to express your beliefs and have them accessible to the
public.

The bottom line: The concept of competition is part of the logic of freedom. Competitions are governed by rules. If you are free to enter the competition, there is no abridgment of freedom. If you lose or are eliminated on the basis of the rules, there is no abridgment of freedom.

Intelligent design was free to enter the competition for a scientific theory of how human beings got here. It does not follow the rules defined by the scientific method and has been eliminated. There is no abridgment of freedom.

Scientists have not been very good at communicating this to the public. Nor have they been effective at explaining the threat to freedom posed by the advocates of intelligent design. It is a threat to the freedom of inquiry into the truth and to the moral imperative of science: to seek the truth without initial bias.

A single consistent logic of contested concepts is not possible. But a logic relating simple uncontested core concepts is possible. *Coercion interferes with freedom* is part of the logic of simple freedom. It uses the simple uncontested version of coercion—the use of force against someone's will. We will call coercion in such a statement an "attendant concept" since it is part of the characterization of simple freedom. Other attendant concepts include harm, rights, justice, fairness, nature, and competition. These attendant concepts act like blanks to be filled in by worldviews, and when not filled in, they are vague.

Simple political freedom is about how simple freedom is affected by taking society into account, having a government, and recognizing social institutions. The logic of simple political freedom has additional attendant concepts—still more blanks to be filled in, as we shall see.

SIMPLE POLITICAL FREEDOM

Simple political freedom begins with the question of how a government can best serve the freedom of its citizens. It further recognizes not just individuals but also institutions: governmental institutions, business institutions, educational institutions, nongovernmental organizations (advocacy groups, think tanks, foundations), religious institutions, political parties, informal groups.

Given the massive political differences in our nation, it is remarkable that there is an uncontested version of political freedom. Political freedom begins with the idea of self-government: Tyrants and dictators can be avoided if we choose those who govern us and make sure that none of them has overriding power. The attendant concepts to simple political freedom are self-government and its democratic institutions—within the national government: Congress, the administration, and an independent judiciary, with a balance of powers and similar structures at lower levels; within civil society: free elections and political parties, a civilian-controlled military, a free market, free press/media, and free religious institutions.

At this level of oversimplification, all of this is uncontested. The details are, however, thoroughly contested: what counts as a balance of power, what is an independent judiciary, when are elections free, what is civilian control of the military, what is meant by a free market. The contestation has been very public: The president has declared a "war on terror" with no end and has taken on war powers indefinitely. He has claimed the authority to spy on American citizens without court orders and to overrule certain laws passed by Congress. Does this upset the balance of power? Is a judiciary independent if a majority of judges are chosen to fit a single political ideology? Is the freedom of a "free market" enhanced or abridged by government regulation, progressive taxation, class action lawsuits, unions, and business-supplied health insurance? Is the air force civilian controlled when the air force academy is controlled by fundamentalist Christians and when the high-ranking military officers are largely conservatives? Is the press free when there is massive media consolidation, when there is little competition among major media outlets, and when control of major media organizations is in the hands of radical conservatives? Is there freedom of religion when fundamentalist evangelicals have gained the power to rewrite the laws of the land and impose their religious beliefs on the nation?

In addition, there are the contributions of government to freedom, both freedom from and freedom to. Freedom from involves protection. Everyone agrees that government should provide protection. But what is protection to mean? Is it military protection, police protection, disaster protection, protection from illness, protection from financial disaster? Is freedom from want included?

Freedom to involves access—access to resources that allow one to achieve one's goals. But what counts as access? Is it access to education (early childhood education and public higher education), access to opportunity (via a federal role in job creation), access to public health institutions, access to the resources on public lands (grazing rights, timber harvesting, mining, oil drilling), access to lucrative government contracts, access to the public treasury (via subsidies and tax breaks)?

A higher-level question governing both cases is this: Should government promote the common good by lumping together the common wealth (taxes) to create a commonly available infrastructure? This is a progressive idea built on the view that we are, and should be, interdependent, that we can't and shouldn't go it alone, that we are all in this together.

Or should the government maximize privatization, building on the conservative idea that everybody is, and should be, on his or her own?

Then there is the role of institutions. Institutions (say, corporations) tend to be viewed metaphorically as people. Which of the rights of people should be guaranteed to corporations? Corporations in other respects act like governments; they rule many aspects of people's lives, but without accountability. Is that democratic?

And what is self-government like? It is agreed that it should maintain order, produce prosperity, and keep records. Is it order produced by authority or order produced by cooperation, responsibility, and trust? Is prosperity to be measured by the assets of the wealthiest, or by the distribution of wealth across income brackets? Is government to be open or secretive? Are its records freely available or locked up?

Finally, how does our national government relate to other governments and to individual people around the world? Does it see itself as part of a world community or as running the world? Does it promote the same freedoms for others around the world as for us?

It should now be clear that there is an uncontested concept of simple political freedom that has a rich collection of oversimplified attendant concepts and a rich logic. It should also be clear that each of these attendant concepts is highly contested.

THE UBIQUITY OF FREEDOM

Finally, there is general agreement on other major ideas and their relation to freedom—at least if one expresses them in uncontested terms.

- *Democracy* is the freedom of a people to govern themselves.
- *Opportunity* is the freedom to take part fully in civil society—to earn a living through work, to participate

in civic organizations, to run for public office, to have access to public accommodations, to get an education, to have a chance at fulfillment in life.

- *Equality* requires the same freedoms for all.
- *Fairness* is when no one has more freedom than anyone else.
- *Education* provides the information needed to sustain freedom and the ability to acquire such information.
- *Health* keeps illness and other bodily harm from impinging on our freedom.
- A *free press* provides free access to the information necessary to preserve freedom.
- The *free market's* proper role is to provide the freedom to engage in trade and to earn a living.
- *Religious freedom* keeps us free from the rule of any church and free to practice any religion, or none.
- *Civilian control of the military* keeps us free from military rule.
- *Academic freedom* allows free inquiry.
- *Personal freedom* defines a realm of "private life," where individuals are free of the state, where the state cannot interfere with individuals pursuing their goals.

Here we can see just why freedom is our most important idea: It is at the center of all other important ideas.

Yet each of these cases is also open to contestation. What counts as being free from the rule of any church? Or from military rule? Or from state interference in private life? In each of these cases, there are very different views of freedom on the part of progressives and radical conservatives.

NEGATING FREEDOM

A crucial aspect of the logic of freedom is what it means to negate freedom. We constantly hear of threats to freedom, attacks on freedom, defending freedom, achieving freedom, spreading freedom, instilling freedom, expanding freedom, losing freedoms, taking our freedoms, regaining freedom, denying freedoms. And with these come ideas like repression, dictatorship, tyranny, oppression, and slavery. How do these enter the basic logic of freedom?

What, for example, is a threat to freedom? It can be a threat of coercion, or harm, or injustice; a threat to security, property, rights, or to the rule of law; or a threat to what is seen as the proper bounds of competition or nature. It can also be seen as a threat to any or all of those things tied to freedom: democracy, opportunity, fairness, equality, education, health, a free press, a free market, civilian control of the military, academic freedom, religious freedom, and personal freedom.

And most important for this book, a threat to free will is a threat to freedom, the imposition of a dangerous worldview without public awareness. When free will itself is threatened, that is the ultimate threat to freedom.

We have just worked through the logic of simple, uncontested freedom. That logic specifies the interactions between the uncontested version of freedom and the uncontested versions of all of the ideas that constitute our understanding of simple freedom: harm, coercion, property, rights, human rights, justice, law, nature, competition, democracy, opportunity, and fairness.

As we have begun to see, *all* of the above concepts are contested. But they tend to be contested in systematic ways—according to the frames of conservative and progressive worldviews, which, we will see, are based on two very different ideas of the family.

PART II

CONTESTED FREEDOM

4

THE NATION-AS-FAMILY METAPHOR

It is hardly surprising that nations are conceptualized metaphorically as families. As children, our first experience of being governed is in our family. We are "ruled" by our parents. We are protected in our homes and told what to do, what rules to follow, how to interact with others, and that we must respect our parents. Our first loyalty, of course, is to our family.

In monarchies, the royal family *is* the government; the king *is* the father. We know about monarchies and other patriarchal forms of government, which means we know about how parents can also be rulers. In the Catholic church—God's Kingdom on Earth—the ruler of the church is called the Holy Father. And countries around the world are called by names such as Mother India, Mother Russia, and the Fatherland.

It should not be a shock that we Americans also conceptualize our nation metaphorically as a family. We have Founding Fathers. We send "our sons and daughters" to war. We have organizations like the Daughters of the American Revolution. Groups in the military think of themselves as "bands of brothers." In America, we have "homeland security," where the nation's landmass is seen as "home" to the nation seen as a "family." And conservatives are clear about the centrality to their politics of "family values."

What is not at all obvious, though, is that the family meta-phor should play a deep conceptual role in our politics—a role so deep that it defines the shape of our politics and the major ideo-logical rift that our nation now faces. And yet, the way we ideal-ize families is central to our politics. In the nation-as-family metaphor, the family corresponds to the nation, the children correspond to adult citizens, and the parent corresponds to a na-tional leader.

Political thought is complex. The range of issues and policies is vast, and new ones arise every day. Yet there is a system that ties people's political views together. There is no objective rea-son why one's views on abortion should have anything at all to do with one's views on taxation, or on environmental regula-tions, or on owning guns, or on tort reform, or on torture. And yet radical conservatives tend to have the same views on all of these. And progressives tend to have the views opposite to those of radical conservatives on all these. What makes these two sets of views hang together?

The answer lies in the fact that Americans have two very dif-ferent models of what an ideal family should be: a strict father family or a nurturant parent family. Whether or not one's real family was like either of these—and real cases do exist by the millions—we all, nonetheless, acquire these ideal models as part of growing up in American culture. They are represented not only in our homes and communities but also in our movies, TV shows, novels, plays, fairy tales, and everyday stories. Strict and nurturant parenting are part of the fabric of everyday culture in America. When these two ideal family models are projected onto the nation by the nation-as-family metaphor, what results are two visions of what our nation should be: The strict father model is the basis of radically conservative politics and the nur-turant parent model informs progressive politics.

As we shall see, the strict father and nurturant parent models are powerful. They not only shape and organize the major political ideologies of our time. They also apply systematically to the uncontested simple, but vague, concept of freedom, filling in the blanks in that concept in two very different ways, to yield two very different—and quite contested—concepts of freedom. It should not be surprising that the same metaphorical ideas—strictness and nurturance—that organize our systems of political thought shape the concepts of freedom that fit into those systems of thought.

The power of these models comes from a number of sources.

- Frames have emotional as well as intellectual content. The difference between strict and nurturant families is not merely structural, but also visceral and powerful because our experiences with our own families and families we have known are highly emotional.
- Those frames govern how we reason.
- A simple family frame can provide the basis for a whole worldview, a way of seeing every aspect of life.
- Metaphors can project the same family-based frames onto different areas of experience—say, economics and religion—organizing these different areas conceptually in the same way.
- Family-based frames and metaphors seem utterly natural and commonsensical—and hence true!
- Family-based frames and metaphors are mostly unconscious, which makes them hard to examine consciously. Their very invisibility gives them power.

It is essential to note that these are idealized models of how a family *should* work—as opposed to how any particular family *does* work. Just about every member of American culture has, in his or her mind, versions of both strict and nurturant models, either actively or passively. Passive versions are not acted on, but rather are used for understanding cultural products like movies, TV shows, and novels. Thoroughgoing progressives use the nurturant model in every active part of their lives and the strict model only passively. Thoroughgoing conservatives use the strict father model in every aspect of their lives and the nurturant model only for understanding cultural products produced by progressives. But many Americans are partial progressives and partial conservatives, using both models actively, though in different parts of their lives.

In the nurturant parent version of the nation-as-family metaphor, the family corresponds to the nation (or community); the children correspond to citizens (who are adults, not children); a nurturant parent corresponds to a national (or community) leader who cares about and acts responsibly toward the citizens; siblings correspond to citizens who care about and act responsibly and empathetically toward each other.

Avoid the trap of taking the metaphor literally. The model says that *the children in the family are mapped to adults in politics*—and that their relationships to political leaders and to each other are metaphorical, not literal, versions of family relationships. These models are part of our common cultural inheritance but may or may not have been realized in a particular person's real family.

Given that we are adults who elect our governments, these family-based models tell us, via metaphor, what kind of governing system we should aim for: one that cares about its citizens and strives to maximize their well-being, or one that seeks to impose its idea of order, rewarding and punishing accordingly, and otherwise seeks to make citizens fend for themselves.

I am *describing* these models, not *proposing* them. To observe the existence of the nation-as-family metaphor in the cognitive unconscious of Americans is not to say that it is good or bad. It is simply there. It shapes our moral systems and our politics. It is not something we can simply change by willing it away.

There are those who think that the brain is infinitely flexible, that we can have whole new minds by simply imagining them, and that it is possible to create whole new social orders just by fiat. It is true that radical conservatives are building—and to a frightening extent have already built—a new social order. But they have done so by tapping what is already in the brains of a great many Americans—the idealized strict father family model—and finding ways to get people to apply it to politics. Building a progressive social order will require the same insight: Start with the nurturant parent model people already use to frame many of their experiences and extend it to politics.

In Chapters 7 and 8, I will describe in detail the nurturant parent and strict father family models and the ways they extend simple, uncontested freedom into two versions of the idea. But before that, I want to review some things to bear in mind as we go through those chapters.

First, the family models are idealized. And they are applied metaphorically. One may use a family-values model metaphorically to structure one's politics without having been brought up that way and without using it for one's own family life. The family model you were brought up with does not necessarily determine how you will operate in your own family or what your politics will be. There are many other factors involved: whether you accepted or rejected your family, your peer group as you were growing up, your education, your work and life experience, a trauma you may have experienced.

Second, real families are more complicated than the ideal models. There are many complex variations on such models. Though it is commonplace for fathers to be strict and mothers to be nurturant, the reverse happens in millions of cases. Do not take the stereotype for the reality. Furthermore, fathers may operate on one model and mothers on another. Thus, many children are brought up with both models simultaneously.

Third, some subcultures have somewhat different models for actually raising their families, but may use these models for politics or other aspects of life.

Fourth, when they are used metaphorically—not literally—these models organize moral and political worldviews. They form the basis, via the nation-as-family metaphor, of coherent and integrated progressive and conservative worldviews. They allow one to explain how disparate political and moral positions on issues fit together and how progressives and conservatives will come down on new issues in given political contexts.

They also explain why a child-rearing organization like Focus on the Family, which teaches strict father child rearing to millions of parents, is politically conservative, why its child-rearing principles, which literally are apolitical, fit a conservative moral and political view of the world.

Fifth, these metaphorical models are *descriptive*, not *prescriptive*. They describe how people *do* think, not how they *should* think.

Sixth, in neither model are citizens of a nation literally treated as children. In both models, the siblings in a family map onto fellow citizens, the family onto the nation, a parent onto the leader of the nation. What is preserved from family to nation are the *values* that define the central relationships in the family. Are the central values empathy, responsibility for oneself and others, and interdependence? Or are they moral authority, discipline, and self-reliance through the individual pursuit of self-interest?

Seventh, these idealized models are mostly unconscious—lived by, used to think with, but often below our awareness. Even though they are unconscious, they can be revealed by various techniques from the cognitive sciences—cognitive analyses, cognitive interviewing, and psychological experiments.

Finally and most important, just about every American has both models engrained in his or her brain, either actively or passively. If you were raised in America, you have been exposed to both models—at least in movies, books, and stories, and on TV. Even if you use only one model in every active part of your life, you can still understand a movie or a story based on the other model. It is in your brain, but used passively for understanding rather than for action.

A great many people are what I call "biconceptuals." They use both models actively—but in different parts of their lives. They may be strict at home but nurturant on the job, or the reverse. There are a lot of blue-collar workers who are strict fathers at home but nurturant in their union politics, and professors who are nurturant at home and in their politics but strict in the classroom. One may be an economic progressive and a social conservative—or an economic conservative and a social progressive. Or one may be a progressive on domestic policy and a neoconservative on foreign policy.

What I find scary in the current situation, as an advocate of dynamic progressive freedom, is that the radical right is using its message machine to move people more and more toward a thoroughgoing conservatism, toward using the strict father model in all aspects of life and politics. What is "extremist" in thoroughgoing conservatism is turning the clock back on the grand expansions of American freedom.

Though the history of our country is progressive overall, there have always been partial conservatives—financial, social, and religious. There have also always been pragmatists—partially progressive and partially conservative in various ways, but wanting things to work: our economy, our educational system, our public health system, our system of national parks. The radical conservatives are reducing the number of pragmatists.

The radical conservative movement has not merely formed coalitions among the various types of conservatives; it is creating a real ideological movement based on strict father morality and the conservative version of freedom. By having a single system of values and their own idea of freedom, radical conservatives are slowly but surely creating an overall fusion of types of conservatives: a blend of the libertarian, financial, social, religious, and neoconservative.

What permits this fusion of types of conservatives is the application of a strict father model to more and more domains of life—personal life, religion, economics, social life, global politics. As the strict father model becomes applied by individuals to more and more aspects of life, the traditional American progressive idea of freedom shifts toward a radically conservative view of freedom.

5

PROGRESSIVE FREEDOM: THE BASICS

What I am calling progressive freedom is simply freedom in the American tradition—the understanding of freedom that I grew up with and have always loved about my country. America has always been a progressive country, and the progressive ideal of freedom has been cherished, defended, and extended over more than two centuries. What contemporary conservatives call freedom, as we shall see, is a radical departure and threatens freedom as we have known it.

DYNAMIC FREEDOM

Progressive freedom is dynamic freedom. Freedom is realized not just in stasis, or at a single moment in history, but in its expansion over a long time. You cannot look only at the Founding Fathers and stop there. If you do, it sounds as if they were hypocrites: They talked liberty but permitted slavery; they talked democracy but allowed only white male property owners to vote. But from a dynamic progressive perspective, the great ideas were expandable freedoms: expanding civil rights, voting rights, property rights, tolerance, education, science, public health, workers' rights, protected parkland, and the infrastructure for progressive freedom—the banking system, court system, transportation system, communication system, university system, scientific research system, social services system, and all the other aspects of the common good that we use our common wealth for. Expanding and deepening the ideas of the Founding Fathers is what dynamic progressive freedom is about.

Progressives don't look backward to before these freedoms were extended to some "original" nascent idea frozen in time, and they don't work to reverse these freedoms as radical conservatives do. As times change, freedoms must expand—or they will contract. Freedom doesn't stand still. Radical conservatives are not going away. If progressives do not keep expanding American freedoms, radical conservatives will contract them.

FREEDOM, PROGRESSIVE STYLE

Progressive freedom is simple freedom, with the vague parts filled in by the progressive worldview. The progressive worldview, I argue, is organized around the nurturant parent model of the family, which centers on empathy, responsibility, and strength. To see how this works, let us look at the nurturant parent model.

THE NURTURANT PARENT MODEL

In this model, both parents (if there are two) are equally responsible. There is no gender hierarchy. The job of a parent is to nurture his or her children, and to raise the children to be nurturers of others! Nurturance involves empathy and responsibility (for both oneself and others), as well as everything that responsibility requires: strength, competence, endurance, and so on.

Nurturant parenting is the opposite of permissive parenting, since it stresses caring about others, responsibility for oneself, and responsibility for others.

Nurturant parents are authoritative without being authoritarian. That is, because they are responsible for and to their children, they become competent parents, learning what they need to learn, and earn the respect of their children—in part by respecting the children. They set fair and reasonable limits and rules, and take the trouble to explain and discuss those limits and rules with their children.

From empathy and responsibility, all progressive values, both within and outside the family, follow:

Security: Security has two aspects, attachment and protection.

Attachment: This is a positive connection, based on unquestioned caring, between child and parent. Politically, attachment is a positive connection between citizen and nation, based on an understanding that the nation cares about its citizens and citizens care about their nation and each other. This is progressive patriotism. Political attachment is the spirit of union we felt all over America right after 9/11, the spirit quickly destroyed by the Bush administration.

Protection: Parents who empathize with their children protect them fiercely. Families make sure their children are protected; in politics, nations make sure their citizens are protected. Protection is a major progressive theme: worker protection, consumer protection, environmental protection, disaster relief, and safety nets—as well as police and military protection.

Fairness: If you care about your child, you want him or her to be treated fairly. Similarly, political leaders who care about their citizens want them to be treated fairly.

Happiness and fulfillment: Unhappy, unfulfilled people tend not to want others to be happier and more fulfilled than they are. Empathy therefore requires that parents be happy and fulfilled, and that they work to make their children that way.

Freedom and opportunity: To be fulfilled, a child has to be free, sufficiently independent to find his or her own way in life. Because of the link between freedom and property, freedom to pursue one's dreams requires opportunity, sufficient access to a job (a means of acquiring property) or to education (which allows you to get property).

General prosperity: Opportunity for all, correspondingly, requires general prosperity spread evenly enough to afford everyone freedom to realistically seek one's own fulfillment in life.

Community: In a nurturant community, leaders care about citizens and act responsibly toward them, and citizens care about their community and each other and act responsibly toward their community and each other. Such a community requires *cooperation*, which requires *trust*, which requires *honesty and openness*. This is true both of the family and of politics.

That is the nurturant parent model of the family and how, in overly simple terms, it structures basic progressive values. We can see immediately some of what it says about progressive freedom:

- Freedom is necessary for fulfillment in life.
- Freedom requires opportunity. Freedom doesn't exist, or is extremely diminished, in the absence of opportunity—say, in extreme poverty. This is akin to Franklin D. Roosevelt's freedom from want.
- Security is required for freedom. This is Roosevelt's freedom from fear.

THE COMMONWEALTH PRINCIPLE: THE INFRASTRUCTURE OF FREEDOM

A nurturant family uses its resources for the good of the family as a whole—for the common good—so that each member can have the freedom to pursue his or her individual goals. The parents may put aside money for the education of the children, or to get a nicer home, or a new family car, or for a down payment on a home for a grown child, or to enable one of the parents to make a career change, or for a disabled child's medical expenses. So that family members can be free to fulfill their needs or their dreams, the family's common wealth is often necessary.

There is a version of this at the heart of progressive politics, an idea as old in America as the colonies: pooling the common wealth for the common good so that individuals can have the resources to be free to pursue their individual goals. That is why there are names for states like the Commonwealth of Massachusetts and the Commonwealth of Virginia. The idea is that a—and perhaps the—central role of government is to use the common wealth for the common good to make individual freedom possible. The common wealth builds the infrastructure for freedom.

Think of all the ways that individual freedom is made possible by that infrastructure, by the use of the common wealth for the common good.

- Physical security: Firefighters for fires, the police for order, the army for defense, FEMA and the national guard for disasters and emergencies, the criminal justice system. Physical security is required for freedom—freedom from fear.
- Family security: Medicare and Medicaid, Social Security, food stamps, unemployment insurance, disability insurance, public housing, homeless shelters. Family security allows family members freedom from want.
- Public health: Food inspections, the Food and Drug Administration, the Centers for Disease Control. Public health provides freedom from harm via disease, unhealthy food, and dangerous pharmaceuticals.

The following allow for freedom to travel and communicate, as well as the freedom to engage in business, and more generally to pursue one's goals.

- Transportation: highways and bridges, public transit, the training of airline pilots (in the air force), the Federal Aviation Administration.
- Communication: the development of the Internet and satellite systems, the regulation of the airwaves by the Federal Communications Commission.
- Public education and government loans for college: needed by business for an educated workforce, and by individuals for fulfillment in life: an understanding of the world, a full appreciation of citizenship, and careers.
- Government funding for research and development: Many computer, space, and medical technologies originated with federally sponsored research.
- Banking and finance: the federal and state banking systems, the Small Business Administration, the Commerce Department, the Federal Trade Commission.
- The courts: mostly used for corporate law, contract disputes, etc.
- Stock market regulation: the Securities and Exchange Commission, etc.

No business can start or function at all without the use of the common wealth, because just about all businesses rely on bank loans, courts to guarantee contracts, the SEC to regulate the stock market, the Internet, cell phones, roads to transport goods, airplanes for travel, universities for research and trained employees. It is part of the genius of America to pool our resources in the name of individual freedom to pursue our needs and dreams. The economy cannot function without the progressive institution of the commonwealth.

A significant part of our common wealth is our common property—our parks and public lands, public areas in cities, our national forests and national monuments, our oceans and rivers, our aquifers, our public beaches, our air, and our airwaves. Maintaining this common property is essential to maintaining individual freedom.

ENVIRONMENTAL FREEDOM

Much of environmentalism is about what I call "environmental freedom," which arises from the empathy and responsibility that define nurturant morality. It is the freedom to connect empathetically with the natural world, the freedom experienced out in nature—in the woods, on snowy mountains, in the desert, at the beach, rafting downriver, sailing, or just walking or playing in a city park. Think of all the ads—for cars, for credit cards—that offer the viewer freedom in nature as a commodity. It is a form of *freedom to*. We are animals who evolved in the natural world. Our animal nature is a major part of who we essentially are, part of our identity. In the natural world, we are free to experience an aspect of our nature, free to be what we most essentially are.

The flip side of this *freedom to* is a *freedom from*—freedom from the impositions of industrialization; from the noise, pollution, and crowds of cities; from jobs that keep one indoors at a desk for long hours; from the sprawl of monotonous suburbs; from advertisements; from the wasteland of TV and radio; from the less wonderful aspects of civilization: war, crime, unscrupulous businesses, and all the rest.

Another form of environmental freedom is environmental health. We are harmed by the pollution of our air and water, mercury in the fish we eat, chemical poisons in our everyday lives—in cosmetics, vinyl, glue that holds down rugs, paint and varnish, cleaning fluids. As we have seen, harm interferes with freedom. Cleaning up our environment and building with green materials is in the service of freedom from environmental harm.

Environmental harm, of course, is not just harm to us via the environment. It is also harm to the environment itself—harm to habitats and the species that need them to live, harm to frogs and fish and animals, harm to animal corridors, to rivers, to forests, to wetlands. Harm to the environment means less freedom to connect with nature and to sense who you are as an animal and where you came from evolutionarily. Harm to the environment also runs counter to empathy and responsibility for the natural world, and is destructive of the common wealth of future generations.

Environmental freedom is achieved through the common-wealth principle, which is implicit in the progressive worldview, shaping our understanding of virtually every political issue. Because it is unconscious, it is not overtly stated, though it forms the basis of a great deal of progressive thought and is implicit in a wide range of policies.

Most of the common wealth comes in the form of taxes. In feudal and colonial times, taxes were imposed by kings and nobles, who took a share of what the common people worked for and earned so they could pay for their lifestyles and support their armies. It is this view of taxation that the American colonists rebelled against. The kings and nobles were taking their property by force or intimidation. Property meant freedom and a loss of property meant an imposition on freedom. In the royal government frame, which characterized our understanding of government by kings and nobles, the benefits went to the kings and nobles, not to those who paid the taxes. Taxes in that frame were indeed an imposition on freedom, except to the extent that the king's armies protected you.

The reverse is true under the commonwealth principle: Citizens, who govern themselves, tax themselves collectively and receive the benefits, benefits coming from the pooling of resources—benefits far greater than their individual tax money, spent one person at a time, could possibly pay for. Fairness is seen as the principle that each should pay according to benefits derived, with higher tax rates for the wealthy than for the poor.

The commonwealth principle is about taxation and the role of the state, which are absolutely required for freedom from a progressive perspective. Taxation pays to create and maintain the commonwealth, which makes freedom possible. Political freedom is not just about protection—from enemies, criminals, and the state itself. It is also about how the state builds the infrastructure of freedom.

The common good is, furthermore, seen as being served when the common wealth is used to make sure that everyone is as free as possible from want and fear. The basis for this, as discussed below, is empathy.

This is the traditional American idea that has been challenged seriously only recently in the radical conservative movement.

FROM SIMPLE FREEDOM TO PROGRESSIVE FREEDOM

It is now time to show how the nurturant parent model fills in the blanks in the overly vague simple freedom model to yield progressive freedom. Here are the blanks subject to contestation from Chapter 3:

Harm: Harm comes in many forms—physical harm, poverty, discrimination, illness, lack of education, pollution, joblessness, and so on.

Coercion: Freedom from being coerced to do things that are for neither your good nor the public good. (Don't impose.)

Property: Wealth and other forms of property can bring one freedom of many kinds. Correspondingly, failure to be paid fairly for the work contribution one makes to society can greatly restrict one's freedom.

The infrastructure of freedom is used by the wealthy more

than by anyone else. The wealthy therefore have by no means earned all their property by themselves; the infrastructure of freedom, paid for by Americans in general, provided them much of their property, and they have a responsibility to pay other Americans back for the use of that infrastructure, and to maintain it in the future for others.

Correspondingly, low income workers do essential labor to uphold the lifestyles of upwards of three-quarters of Americans. They work for a living but do not earn a living. They have earned more than they are being paid and deserve a bonus from the economy as a whole.

Security: Protection is a progressive value—physical protection, as well as consumer protection, worker protection, safety nets, etc. Protection from harm contributes to freedom.

Rights: Empathy and responsibility lead one to care about, and act to advance, the civil and legal rights, and hence the freedom, of oneself and others.

Human rights: Empathy leads one to inalienable rights—the right to the basic things people need to survive and thrive, and experience basic freedoms.

Justice: Nurturant morality stresses restitution over retribution whenever possible—especially for nonviolent people, the idea of rehabilitation over punishment for punishment's sake.

Responsibility for freedom: Responsibility (for both oneself and others) is a central nurturant value. Freedom is maximized when the members of a society take responsibility for the freedom of others. Freedom is lost when corporations carry out governing functions on a private basis, driven by profit, not responsibility, without accountability to the public. Privatization is thus to be disfavored whenever corporations might take on a function governing the lives and well-being of citizens.

Order: People cannot function freely in physical, social, or political chaos—as our experience in Iraq shows all too painfully. Empathy requires that people be able to function, which requires

an orderly society. Responsibility requires that each citizen contribute to that order—except in the case where nonviolent civil
disobedience is overwhelmingly required for the sake of central
freedoms.

The rule of law: Empathy requires the protection of the law
—for freedom not only from physical harm but also from the
harmful effects of unscrupulous or irresponsible corporations.
Prevention of harm is preferable. Harm interferes with freedom.
That's why policing and government regulations that prevent
harm serve the cause of freedom.

Where harm has occurred at the hands of an individual, the
courts are needed to isolate the harmful person from the community, to rehabilitate the harmful person when possible, to punish
so as to act as a deterrent in those cases where a deterrence effect
is real, and/or to assign restitution, where there has been no violence or harm to others.

Where harm has occurred at the hands of a corporation, the
civil justice system is required in order to guarantee that substantial compensatory and punitive damages are paid by the guilty
defendant in order to provide financial compensation to victims,
financial deterrence to corporate wrongdoers, and payment to
civil justice attorneys both for legal services rendered and for doing the work of the police and the prosecutor. Without substantial damages paid out to law firms, the system will break down
because lawyers will no longer be able to function as police and
prosecutors.

Nature: Natural forces don't count as interfering with freedom. Markets are not seen as natural; they are man-made for certain interests and not others. Markets can harm people when
they are constructed for the interests of others.

Since empathy and responsibility imply protection, failure to
offer adequate protections from or assistance after natural forces
does count for progressives as interfering with freedom. For example, prior to Hurricane Katrina, the Bush administration, as a

matter of conservative political policy, redirected levee repair funds to provide a tax break for the wealthy and to fund the Iraq War; ignored class-five hurricane warnings based on global-warming research; weakened, demoted, and defunded FEMA so that it could not respond quickly and forcefully to a class-five hurricane on the gulf. These were human causes, not natural causes, of the Katrina disaster and hence interfered with the citizens' freedom.

Competition: Winning competitions is not seen as harming other competitors and thereby restricting their freedom. But competitions must be freely entered into by all parties, and their rules must be fair—as empathy and responsibility require. Otherwise, the competition frame is not met and "winning" may be harming others and thereby restricting their freedom.

So-called free-trade agreements often violate these conditions for competition. These agreements are often unfair, having been negotiated to the advantage of U.S. corporations, leaving out the consent of the individuals governed, especially indigenous populations, subsistence farmers, and factory workers in third-world countries.

The agreements have often had the effect of making it impossible for indigenous populations to continue supporting themselves, forcing farmers off the land and into cities where they have no alternative to working in poverty, with horrendous labor conditions. They have also had the effect of outsourcing American jobs to other countries, lowering wage scales here, and forcing more Americans into the cheap labor trap. When this occurs, so-called free-trade agreements in the name of competition work against freedom both here and abroad.

Self-government: The government should care about citizens and accept the responsibility to maximize their freedom while maintaining social responsibility.

Openness: Freedom is best served when the government is open and honest, and works by trust.

Fairness and equality: The government should empathize with those in need. The vastly unequal distribution of income and assets is undemocratic. Those who have more should contribute more. Political equality means that money and the influence that goes with it should be taken out of politics.

These examples should show in detail how the values of the nurturant parent model apply to simple freedom and fill in the blanks to arrive at a concept of progressive freedom. In each case, the central progressive values of empathy and responsibility flesh out a progressive interpretation of concepts like harm, security, nature, and competition, extending simple freedom to progressive freedom. The result is a systematic extension: The same nurturant parent model extends all the concepts uniformly.

In Chapters 8–11, we will examine how the strict and nurturant models apply to extend simple freedom in much greater detail for four cases: personal freedom, economic freedom, religious freedom, and freedom in foreign policy.

EMPATHY AND FREEDOM

Empathy forms the basis for the progressive worldview. It is empathy that makes us concerned about the freedom of others.

It is no accident that the nurturant parent model begins with empathy. Progressive morality is centrally about empathy.

We are born wired for empathy. Our brains come with the neural circuitry. One piece of the circuitry is the mirror neuron system, a structure of neural connections linking the premotor cortex (which "choreographs" complex movements) and the parietal cortex (which integrates sensory information). Through experience, the mirror system appears to become "tuned" to link

the control of one's actions with the perceptions of others performing those actions. Neurons in the mirror system fire when
you perform an action or perceive someone else performing the
same action. That is how you can imitate an action or tell when
someone is doing the same thing that you are.

Another piece of circuitry links the mirror system to the
emotional centers of the brain. This circuitry is responsible for
the physiology of emotion—the muscles in your face and body
whose activity correlates with being happy, sad, angry, afraid, or
disgusted. The physiology of the emotion system and the mirror
system operating together enable you to tell what emotions others are feeling—or apparently feeling, if they are good actors.
Many scientists believe that these systems, working together, are
the physiological basis for empathy—for connecting us to others,
both people and animals, and to the world. It is through empathy that we can "mind read," that is, feel someone's pain and joy,
tell what others are feeling and what they are in the midst of
doing.

Though we come wired for it, that neural wiring still has to
be developed and used or it can decay or fail to develop further.
Feeling someone's pain and joy—feeling what another feels—is
the mark of empathy.

Empathy is at the center of progressive values. Caring about
others as well as yourself is at the heart of the value system. Its
natural companion is responsibility, the responsibility to help—
to act on your empathy. Empathy without responsibility is hollow. It would be like identifying with a crying child but doing
nothing about what made her cry—not trying to alleviate her
hunger, fear, or frustration. In the progressive worldview, progressives, as citizens, should be both empathetic and responsible.

Empathy and responsibility combine to characterize the relationship between the common good and individual freedom.
Empathy for those in need—connection to them as fellow human beings—requires us to have a form of government that is

"*for* the people." Empathy leads to fairness and equality as values. Responsibility for others requires that we do more than express compassion, that we act on these values and respond to another's suffering. And responsibility for oneself—the idea that you cannot take care of others if you don't take care of yourself—leads to a serious consideration of how self-interest balances with other values.

Empathy also places an important constraint on freedom.

The consideration principle: The exercise of your freedom should not interfere with the freedom of others.

It is immoral to harm, enslave, or deny the fulfillment of others through the exercise of your freedom. This is a central principle of progressive thought. Consideration for the freedom of others is a progressive moral mandate. Consideration of others, when applied only to individuals, sounds like a limitation. But when applied to everyone, it becomes an optimization principle, because others would be applying it to *you*—working to guarantee you as much freedom as possible. It is a form of the Golden Rule.

The consideration principle (generalized): Everyone gains more freedom when everyone interferes the least with the freedom of others.

This is a central component of the progressive notion of a free society. But it is only half of the story, the empathy half, which is about freedom from—from the interference of others. The responsibility half has to do with positive action, not just noninterference. Empathy says that because you want to be free, you, as an empathetic person, will want others to be free as well. Responsibility says that you have a moral requirement to act on your empathy—a responsibility to act to help make others free as well. That is what social responsibility is all about. Empathy plus responsibility together entail a broader principle than the mere consideration principle.

The responsibility-for-freedom principle: Everyone becomes most free when everyone acts positively to maximize the freedom of others.

This, of course, includes not interfering with the freedom of others. But it goes much further. Social responsibility requires positive action to ensure the freedom of others, rather than passively not interfering with it. This too is central to the traditional American approach to freedom. It arises from empathy plus responsibility—the defining values of nurturant parenting. It is because Americans have adopted the responsibility-for-freedom principle that so many progressive freedoms have been expanded over the generations. It is because Americans have traditionally taken responsibility for freedom that freedom has been progressive and dynamic.

THE FREEDOM MOVEMENTS

For me, the proudest moments in American history have been our gains in freedom. It began with America's independence from the rule of King George III and the establishment of a democracy—beautiful, but with imperfections. We gained freedom from external authoritarian rule, but there was still freedom to be gained at home. The freeing of the slaves was a momentous step. Woman suffrage followed, freeing women to vote. And the establishment of the national park system was a great step forward in environmental freedom.

The New Deal was a milestone: Crucial freedoms—freedom from want and fear—were deepened by extending the use of the common wealth for the common good in the name of freedom. The labor movement, freeing working people from the authoritarian economic domination of big business over individual workers, championing and getting the eight-hour day and five-day week, fairer wages, and benefits. The defeat of fascism—

overcoming the idea that some races and nationalities are inherently better than others and should rule those that are "inferior" by brute force, slaughtering those deemed so inferior they do not even have a right to live. The fascist idea is the very opposite of America's responsibility-for-freedom principle.

Then came the great freedom movements of the '60s and '70s—advancing freedoms for racial and ethnic minorities and women, and the environmental movement that made enormous progress in all areas of environmental freedom. Another move toward freedom was the recognition of past outrages against freedom by Americans—outrages against our own population, the slaughter of Native Americans and the internment of Japanese Americans.

These are advances made possible by empathy and responsibility. Empathy turns the visceral sense of another's lack of freedom into your lack of freedom. Responsibility calls on you to do something about it. What goes with responsibility—strength, competence, and endurance—has mattered greatly as well: the strength and competence of those who built the freedom movements and their endurance over decades to keep fighting in the face of great hurdles. These freedom movements, and the people who created and sustained them, have made me most proud to be an American.

E pluribus unum, the ideal of a united America, is made possible through empathy, which connects us to each other and insists that freedom for me is possible only if there is freedom for you. We saw a revival of this ideal just after September 11, 2001, when all Americans were New Yorkers, and New Yorkers—as well as those who flocked to New York to help—showed not a hollow empathy but a progressive empathy made real by responsibility, strength, competence, and endurance.

TYPES OF PROGRESSIVES,
TYPES OF FREEDOM

There are six basic kinds of progressives, based on the principal modes of progressive thought, each with its own basic understanding of freedom.

SOCIOECONOMIC PROGRESSIVES

Freedom is fundamentally social, political, and economic in character. It consists in sufficient social, political, and economic resources to enjoy basic freedoms:

- Pay in proportion to contributions to society through work
- Equality of social and political power
- A baseline of property sufficient to live a healthy life with basic needs met
- A baseline of social capital sufficient to function effectively in society
- Sufficient collective economic power to bargain effectively for wages and benefits

The labor movement has historically been central to these concerns, as has the antipoverty movement and other social justice movements.

In the international arena, socioeconomic progressives have seen foreign policy as fulfilling the UN Declaration of Human Rights in the UN Charter. Accordingly, they have turned their attention to human-level issues: human rights in general; women's rights and population issues (governed by the level of women's education and participation in society); the international slave and sex trade; global public health and environmental issues; third-world development, poverty, and hunger;

genocide, political violence, and refugee issues; the rights of indigenous peoples to maintain their traditional culture. In the service of these concerns, they have looked to international cooperation across nations, to international organizations concerned with these issues; and to person-to-person interventions (for example, Doctors Without Borders).

In the arena of Islamic terrorism, socioeconomic progressives have promoted nonviolent forms of international cooperation and intervention: cutting off financing for radical Islamic schools and offering free educational alternatives, promoting alternatives in popular culture, religion, and education to radical Islam; promoting women's rights and education in Islamic countries; promoting economic development in places where that could curb a culture of terrorism. They have also promoted sensible forms of homeland security—security of ports, containerized shipping, railroads, chemical factories, and nuclear power plants—as well as strengthening responders like firefighters and police.

IDENTITY-POLITICS PROGRESSIVES

They are members of, or represent, groups that have been or currently are oppressed, economically and socially. They seek redress, as well as recognition for their diverse contributions to culture.

ENVIRONMENTAL PROGRESSIVES

They support the promotion and preservation of environmental freedom in all its forms:

- Freedom of connection with the natural world
- Freedom from environmental harm
- Freedom from destructive impositions of industrialization

This requires preservation and extension of common property (parks and preserves, rivers, oceans, and wetlands); protection of species and their habitats; protection from pollution and poisoning; and the maximal separation of the built-up and natural landscapes.

CIVIL LIBERTIES PROGRESSIVES

Freedoms here are the basic political liberties: freedom of speech, the press, information, assembly, and religion; protection of rights: voting rights, right to a fair trial, right to privacy, equal rights before the law; the right to earn a living—get a job without discrimination, to start a business, and so on.

Progressive libertarians focus on or campaign for such things as freedom to copy files over the Internet and free use of certain forms of intellectual property: computer operating systems; computer programs; artistic products such as music, videos, movies, newspaper and journal articles. They also campaign for protection of private information on the Internet or in computer files.

SPIRITUAL PROGRESSIVES

In traditional Western religions—Judaism, Christianity, and Islam—God is seen as a nurturant parent, offering unconditional love with a nurturant morality, and calling for empathy with responsibility for those less able to take care of themselves. Spiritual freedom lies not in heaven but living a moral life on earth.

Some spiritual progressives have no notion of God as a person (Buddhists, Taoists) or no religion at all. What makes them spiritual progressives is a nurturant morality that calls for an empathetic connection with others and with the physical world that includes a commitment to an alleviation of suffering in oneself and others.

ANTIAUTHORITARIAN PROGRESSIVES

Nurturant morality shuns the illegitimate use of power over others to gain advantage or to harm. Antiauthoritarian progressives focus on freedom from such illegitimate uses of power, whether by government, corporations, religions, or individuals, in all areas of life.

For example, the antiwar movement focuses on the illegitimate use of military power and inhuman military weaponry, such as nuclear weapons. The business ethics movement focuses on the power of corporations to harm. The means used is public shame—shame on the administration for starting a war on false pretenses, using tactics that impose large numbers of casualties on innocent civilians, and using torture; and shame on corporations for producing products that harm consumers or the general public.

IDEALISTS, PRAGMATISTS, AND MILITANTS

In addition to these six modes of thought, there are five types of progressive attitudes. Some progressives are idealists, unwilling to compromise their principles and unwilling to accept half measures. Some are pragmatists, who want to optimize their principles but are willing to compromise in order to get things to work. Some are real-world pragmatists, who want the economy to function, the educational system to teach children, the health system to keep us well, the Social Security system to keep people out of poverty in old age. They are willing to compromise their principles when their principles are at odds with how the world works. Some are political pragmatists, who want to maximize their political clout and are willing to compromise their principles for that purpose.

Finally, there are militants. Militants distinguish means and ends. They have nurturant ends; their goals are progressive. But they have strict father means. For example, they may have antiauthoritarian principles but run their organizations in an authoritarian way. As men, they may fight for feminist principles but are patriarchal in their personal lives, insisting that they alone set the rules. They may be peace activists but engage in violent protests for the sake of peace.

Authoritarian antiauthoritarians may logically contradict each other, but pure logic isn't at issue in the human brain. They are using two different logics—strict and nurturant—for what is to them two different conceptual arenas: means and ends. It is no more contradictory from a cognitive perspective than conservatives who are both pro-life and pro–death penalty.

Progressives tend to be divided by issues, modes of thought, and attitude. They focus on their differences more than their similarities. Conservatives are much more effective in coming together. What unites them cognitively is strict father morality and their view of freedom. Progressives have an overall cognitive and moral vision that is just as unified, and just as coherent a view of freedom, but it mostly remains unconscious. It has not been made explicit and articulated to themselves and others. If we progressives continue to dote on difference and insist on individuality rather than a common vision, we will let the conservatives take freedom from us—not just the word but also the idea and the reality.

6

CONSERVATIVE FREEDOM: THE BASICS

It is time to begin our discussion of what the radical right means by freedom. It is important at the outset to note how very often right-wing Republicans use the words "freedom" and "liberty." If their version of freedom and liberty were generally recognized, they would not have to. They could just assume that everyone recognized that they were the natural inheritors of those ideas. The reason they have to say "freedom" and "liberty" over and over is that the progressive versions of those ideas have always dominated American life, and it is the progressive versions that Americans still hold in their hearts. Republican radicals call themselves "conservatives" to try to convince the rest of the country that their view of freedom, built upon their values, is really the traditional American one. The fact is that their idea of freedom is radical and outside the mainstream of American history and American life today.

When they talk about freedom and liberty, they assume that they are not free and are oppressed. Who are they oppressed by? Americans. Americans who view freedom as most Americans always have.

THE STRICT FATHER FAMILY MODEL

The radical right, or "conservative," view of freedom can be seen as arising from simple freedom with the blanks filled in by the conservative worldview. That worldview is structured, as conservatives regularly point out, by family values—in particular, the values of the strict father family applied to politics via the nation-as-family metaphor.

The strict father family is, like the nurturant parent family, an idealization of family life, a cognitive model that serves as an ideal. In the strict father family, the major elements of the conservative worldviews are structured as an organic whole. It is that organic whole that makes the conservative worldview fit together.

THE STRICT FATHER FAMILY

There are two parents, a father and a mother. Morally, there is absolute right and absolute wrong. The strict father is the moral authority in the family; he knows right from wrong, is inherently moral, and has the authority to be head of the household. A family needs a strict father because:

- The family should be run on a moral basis and the authority should be a moral authority. The authority of the father must not be seriously challenged.
- There is evil in the world, and the family needs a father strong enough to protect it from evil.
- There is competition in the world. There will always be winners and losers. To support the family, a father has to be able to win in a competitive world.
- Children are born bad, in the sense that they want to do whatever feels good, not what's right. They need a strict father to teach them right from wrong. Moral ac-

tion is obedience to the moral authority, the father. Children learn right from wrong and become moral beings in only one way: punishment when they do wrong—punishment painful enough, either physically or psychologically, to give them an incentive to do right. Only in that way will they develop the internal discipline needed to function as moral beings. Such punishment is seen as an expression of love and is called tough love.

- The authority should be the father, since "Mommy" is not strong enough to protect the family, not able to win competitions and support the family, and not strict enough to discipline the children sufficiently.

- The mother's role is to uphold the authority of the father, take care of the household, and comfort the children when they need it.

- Affection is important, either as a reward for obedience or to prevent alienation through a show of love despite painful punishment.

- Discipline has an important secondary effect. If you are disciplined, you can pursue your self-interest to become prosperous.

- The mechanism for this is a version of free-market capitalism: If everybody pursues his or her own self-interest, then the self-interests of all will be maximized, as a law of nature (as Adam Smith said, by the invisible hand). It is therefore moral to pursue your self-interest, since by doing so you are helping everyone.

- Correspondingly, it is wrong to give people things they haven't earned, since it will take away their incentive to be disciplined, which will make them dependent and less capable of acting morally. It is also wrong to take away the rewards of discipline, since it removes the incentive to be disciplined.

- Since both morality and prosperity come from self-

discipline, morality correlates with prosperity. If you're
not disciplined enough to be prosperous, you're not
disciplined enough to be moral, so you deserve your
poverty. This creates a natural hierarchy of morality
paired with wealth and power. In a well-ordered world,
those in authority should be the moral people, since
they deserve to be in authority.

- Mature children should ideally have become sufficiently disciplined to function on their own, support
themselves, and be their own moral authorities. At
that point, they are their own moral authorities, free of
obedience to the strict father, and from then on he
should not "meddle" in their lives.
- A mature child who is not sufficiently disciplined is
never coddled but needs more tough love and so is sent
out to face the discipline of the world.

Ideally, the father will protect and support the family, exercise his authority well, and raise disciplined, moral, well-
behaved, obedient children who can prosper in the world and
form their own strict father families. He will never coddle or
spoil his children, never show weakness or indecision, never
yield his authority, never allow himself to be manipulated. This
is tough love, but it *is* what love is in this model.

That is the ideal model. In real families, the model fails on its
own terms when the father goes over the line—when he is abu-
sive, unrealistic, lies to hide disturbing truths, betrays the family's trust, weakens the family, gets the family into financial
trouble, or harms and alienates the children. This happens often
enough to be a recognized social phenomenon. Strict father families have high rates of spousal and child abuse and divorce.

The strict father model of the family unites many themes into
an intuitive seamless whole and, via the nation-as-family
metaphor, structures right-wing politics in terms of the politi-

cal version of those themes. The themes, translated into political terms, are

- The naturalness and primacy of the moral system itself.
- The unchallengeable moral authority of the leader.
- Morality as obedience to moral authority.
- The fight against evil. Evil resides not just in the threat of harm, but especially in the rejection of the moral system itself. ("They hate our freedoms.")
- Behavior as naturally governed by rewards and punishments.
- Discipline as the basis of morality.
- Discipline as the basis of prosperity and power.
- Discipline as the basis for winning in competitive situations.
- The free market as the mechanism of fair competition— the mechanism by which those who are moral, and hence disciplined, can become prosperous and thus be rewarded.
- The natural link between morality and wealth and power.
- The moral order—the hierarchy of authority and wealth is a moral hierarchy.
- Freedom as the means to achieving one's own moral authority.
- Freedom as the means to achieving wealth and power.

The strict father family model is a mechanism for running a family and raising children. Beyond that, it organizes and makes sense of these moral, economic, and political themes, and contributes to a society that is organized according to those themes.

NURTURANT CONSERVATIVE
COMMUNITIES

It is extremely common in the American Midwest for political conservatives on national issues to want to live in a nurturant community. In an ideal nurturant community, the community leaders care about the community members and are responsible to and for them, and community members do community service, care about each other, respect each other, and act responsibly to help each other. Many conservatives in America prefer to live in such a community rather than in a strict father community, where there is a community leader who runs things and you'd better do things his way, or else.

Though there certainly are conservative communities run on a strict father model, it is striking that there is another prominent model for conservative communities: in-group nurturance; out-group strictness. If you accept the community values, develop the requisite discipline, and show loyalty to the values and the community, then you are treated nurturantly. Strict father families can be extremely loving and caring toward children who measure up. Fundamentalist communities can be nurturant and loving toward members who fit in. And even the military, the strictest of institutions, has an internal nurturant creed: Group members are loyal to each other and take care of each other. Families on military bases get housing, good schooling, health care, and low prices at the PX. Conservative think tanks treat their talent well; some pay their interns and have apartments for them. Nurturance in such communities is a reward for doing all the right things. Such communities also show little tolerance for those who do not fit in.

In short, many conservatives prefer to live in a caring community of like-minded people who share strict father morality as a way of life. As long as you go along with the mores of the group, you are treated well, cared about, and, when necessary, cared for. Charity and compassion are important values in such communities, as is hospitality.

A central idea here is the "worthy poor." These people need help and are worth helping—fine, God-fearing people who happen to be down on their luck, wiped out financially by a flood or fire, lost their job, or had an illness. Missionary zeal is for people who have "lost their way"—taken to alcohol or drugs and need rehabilitation—who can be made worthy, usually through fundamentalist religion.

This is, for the most part, real compassion and real charity—but limited. You get to choose who you are charitable toward. It is often not compassionate toward African-American welfare mothers, young girls who have gotten pregnant and want an abortion, gays and others who are not counted as worthy. Being helped through such compassion and charity is very different from being helped just because you are a human being and have a right to be treated as such.

Marvin Olasky, author of *The Tragedy of American Compassion*, is credited with coining the term "compassionate conservative." Like many other conservatives, he sees social programs as immoral—as giving people things they haven't earned, making people dependent on the government, and robbing them of their discipline. True compassion, he says, is tough love—eliminating government social programs and forcing the poor to go out and make it on their own. Only charity that is directly personal, requires the able-bodied to work, and includes explicit spiritual counseling has any hope of success.

THE FUNDAMENTAL FRAMES

Just as the nurturant parent family motivates the commonwealth principle, so the strict father family motivates a set of individualist principles that are the very opposite of the commonwealth principle.

- It's individual initiative that has made this country great.
- The unfettered free market is the engine of American prosperity. It is natural and moral.
- Everyone can pull themselves up by their bootstraps. Responsibility is individual responsibility.
- The government just gets in the way; it is inefficient, bureaucratic, and wasteful.
- It's your money; you can spend it better than the government can.

The good people—the moral ones—are disciplined. They can become prosperous via the market if the government doesn't get in the way. The government can mess up the free market in three ways:

- Government regulation: stopping entrepreneurs from using their own judgment
- Taxation: taking away the incentive to make money by taxing initiative
- Lawsuits: Permitting juries to grant very high awards that threaten the rewards for individual initiative

Freedom here is the freedom to become disciplined, freedom from government interference, and the freedom to enter the free market and become prosperous.

These fundamental frames are repeated over and over until they seem like common sense.

FROM SIMPLE FREEDOM TO
CONSERVATIVE FREEDOM

We are now in a position to see how the strict father model fills in the blanks in simple freedom to yield conservative freedom.

Harm: Freedom from harm is gained through force—the military at the national level, the police at the local level, and your own guns at the individual or family level.

Coercion: Freedom from coercion by the state or by the liberal elite.

Property: Property is your reward for being sufficiently disciplined to be able to be moral. Wealth and other forms of property can bring one freedom of many kinds. You earn your property through the market by being disciplined, or you inherit it from others who earned it. Property rights are absolute. You own your property and should have the freedom to use or dispose of it any way you want. The government should not be able to take your property under any circumstances without fair compensation. Taxation and regulation rob you of your freedom.

Security: Physical security provides freedom from harm by other people, and that is the only legitimate role for the government. Those who provide security to you have legitimate authority over you (the military, Homeland Security, the police). Individuals are responsible for other forms of security—health security, retirement security.

In a strict father family, it is the father who protects you. He has not only the right but also the duty to be aware of where you are and what you are doing. If you are where you're supposed to be and are doing what you're supposed to be doing, there is nothing to fear.

Similarly the security apparatus of the government—the military, intelligence agencies, and the police—have both the right and the duty to keep citizens and their activities under surveillance. Law-abiding citizens have nothing to fear. Security trumps the right to privacy.

Rights: Everyone has the right to carry out moral obligations and to engage in natural human activities. Since we have both the right and the duty to protect ourselves and our families, we have the right to bear arms to do so. Since we have the duty to teach our children right from wrong, we have the right to dictate what their education should be. Since we have a duty to support our families, we have the right to start a business and engage freely in trade.

The Constitution guarantees us freedom of speech and religion. Religion is a natural activity and we have the right to practice our religion freely, openly, and in public. For evangelicals, that means spreading the "good news" to as many people as possible.

Because nature is there to be used by human beings, we have the right to exploit natural resources and engage in development.

To take away such rights would be an imposition on freedom.

Human rights: The rights given above are rights that everyone in every country should have.

Justice: There can be no morality without punishment for harm. Harm is an imposition on freedom. Justice is retribution. The imposition on the freedom of the victim must be matched by an imposition on the freedom of the criminal. Victims and their families can rest only after wrongdoers have been punished severely for severe crimes. Criminals have forfeited their right to freedom. Murderers have forfeited their right to life.

Responsibility for freedom: Responsibility is individual responsibility. Except for military and police protection of our bodies, our property, and our rights, we are responsible for our own freedoms. Every individual is responsible for taking care of himself and his family—for earning enough for food, clothing, shelter, and health care, and for defending his own family. Fundamentalist Christians have a responsibility for playing their part in carry-ing out God's plan. Citizens also have a duty to be loyal to their country and serve their nation, especially the military, which protects the nation from external evils.

Order: People cannot function freely in physical, social, or political chaos. In a strict father family, it is the duty of the fa-ther to maintain order and the duty of others in the family to show respect and do their part. Rowdy demonstrations or disre-spect or disloyalty to the nation, the military, or the police un-dermines legitimate authority, which must be maintained for the sake of both order and protection.

The rule of law: What is legal should accord with what is moral according to strict father morality. Laws that violate morality should be changed and it is our duty to work to change them; for example, laws that make abortion legal. It is the duty of citizens to obey the law and to respect those who administer it, unless they are imposing their own immoral views, as in the case of activist judges.

Nature: Natural forces don't count as interfering with free-dom. For example, Hurricane Katrina was a natural disaster and no one bears any blame for it.

Competition: Normally, freedom comes with the moral obliga-tion not to impose on the freedom of others. But in competition, this moral obligation is lifted, so long as you obey the rules. Win-ners can beat losers in competition without it being seen as an imposition on the losers' freedom. Even if the loser is harmed by the loss, as long as the rules are obeyed, the loss is not considered an imposition on freedom.

Engaging in business is a form of competition; once you are in business, you are not imposing on the freedom of your competi-tors, which frees you to do whatever is necessary to win—within the law. What does restrict freedom in business are limitations on the free market: government regulation, taxes, and lawsuits.

The free market is thus, ideally, about freedom—the freedom

to make money without qualms about interfering with the freedom of others. From this perspective, government, which imposes regulations and taxes and in whose courts lawsuits take place, is interfering with freedom.

TYPES OF CONSERVATIVES

Now that we have shown how the strict father model fills in the blanks in simple freedom to produce conservative freedom, we can make sense of the types of conservatives. Each is a different version of strict father morality, applied to different issue areas.

FINANCIAL CONSERVATIVES

Freedom for financial conservatives flows from private property—the freedom to acquire it, keep it, and use it. They see the free market as natural (people naturally pursue profit) and moral (it maximizes the profit of all). They are against social programs, which they see as seizing their legitimately earned wealth and giving it to people who have not been disciplined enough to earn it, don't deserve it, and are being made dependent on the state.

For them, communism, socialism, the New Deal, and the labor movement are all evils, threats to the laissez-faire free-market system and the ideas that go with it: reward and punishment, competition, discipline, and the moral order. Thus, they support a strong defense against communism, socialism, and radical Islam. And they oppose environmentalism, which they see as restricting the free use of the environment as a resource for profit. In short, they see financial harm as harm that restricts freedom. They accept the corporations as persons metaphor and see anything that threatens profit to corporations as a potential form of harm, restricting the freedom of corporations.

Financial conservatives are often those who own, own stock in, manage, represent, or identify with the owners of large corporations. When those corporations benefit, *they* benefit. They tend to see corporations as citizens—citizens with special status. The country is best run when it is run for the profit—and the freedom of operation—of large corporations. "What's good for General Motors is good for America," as Charles E. Wilson, president of General Motors and Dwight Eisenhower's secretary of defense, said back in 1952.

An important aspect of discipline is fiscal discipline—not spending money one doesn't have, or can't readily get or borrow at reasonable rates. For financial conservatives, very large deficits could ultimately harm business—unless matched by either economic growth, the ability to borrow money cheaply, continuously deferred payments, or the prospect of eliminating the costs of social programs.

LIBERTARIANS

Libertarians focus on being their own moral authorities, free of any strict father's authority. In politics, this means being free of the government's authority.

Libertarians are radical financial conservatives. They see free markets as defining freedom and want to extend the ideas of free markets to replace as many government functions as possible. They prefer privatization of just about everything, except for the "minimal state"—the military and the police, and the basic infrastructure needed to defend the country, protect lives and property, and keep order.

Competition is the basis of the free market, which is the essential engine of freedom. Competition favors the most disci-

plined and defines who is best. Competition thus creates a natural hierarchy of merit, where those who deserve to win do win—
by definition. Losers are just that—losers! Competition, they
believe, should be extended to as many realms of life as possible.
Standards of competition are "standards" for society.

SOCIAL CONSERVATIVES

Strict father morality should govern family life and social life, especially with respect to men's and women's roles. Masculinity is
strict father masculinity. The parents can't be gay in that model,
so gay marriage is a threat. The father controls reproductive decisions in that model, so reproductive rights are a threat. The father is a protector, so gun control is a threat. Freedom comes
from being disciplined and knowing right from wrong—or, even
better, being your own moral authority. Law should also follow
strict father morality. Patriotism lies in maintaining the moral
authority of this nation over other nations. Social programs are
immoral, giving lazy people things they haven't earned, taking
away their discipline, and making them dependent.

FUNDAMENTALISTS

Fundamentalist Christianity starts with the idea that God is a
strict father: You obey his commandments, and you go to heaven
as your reward; otherwise, you are punished with eternal torture
in hell. With Christ, you get a second chance, but again, it's
heaven if you obey and hell if you don't.

Strict father family life and social morality are seen as natural, following from the nature of God as a strict father. Just as
the strict father's word is law in the household, so God's word—
the Bible—should be law on earth.

Fundamentalists are evangelicals; their mission is to convert:

Defending and extending the strict father system in religion and daily life is a moral duty.

Fundamentalists are, of course, social conservatives as well.

Going to your reward—to heaven—is the ultimate freedom. Religion is the path to freedom; politics should be in the service of that freedom. Religious freedom is not in the separation of church and state. It is the freedom to evangelize, to spread the good news, to spread the word of God through school prayer in public as well as religious schools, to put the Ten Commandments in every courthouse because they are God's law, the natural basis of man's law. Freedom *of* religion (to do God's bidding, which is inherently moral and should be legal) is not freedom *from* religion. The separation of church and state is seen as state support for secularism and against true religion, and it therefore is an imposition against religious freedom.

NEOCONSERVATIVES

Neoconservatives are centrally concerned with applying strict father morality to foreign policy. The United States is seen as the moral authority in the world, and it is its moral duty to maintain its sovereignty and to use its military and economic power to maximize American interests, which are, in this view, also the interests of other countries.

Neoconservatives believe in "free-market freedom"—spreading free markets throughout the world, which American corporations can enter and dominate. They take for granted the truth of what I will call "the free market freedom theory," that once free markets take hold, other democratic institutions naturally follow:

- Free elections, so that business leaders can secure their rights (against their property being seized by the government) through a government that optimizes their interests, as opposed to a tyrant who optimizes his own interests

- Checks and balances, to limit the power of any government to control their property and the functioning of any business
- Civil liberties, to limit the power of any government over the lives of those running businesses
- Civilian control of the military, to prevent military coups, which could threaten private property and civil liberties
- A free press, because business depends on many kinds of accurate information

In these ways, neoconservatives assume that strict father morality serves democratic ideals.

Those are the basics of the radical conservative idea of freedom. They arise from using strict father morality to fill in the blanks in simple freedom.

7

CAUSATION AND FREEDOM

I've been wondering for some time about a phenomenon I keep running into—moral or political disputes between progressives and conservatives, where the progressives argue on the basis of systemic causation (within a social, ecological, or economic system) and the conservatives argue on the basis of direct causation (by a single individual).

Examples are everywhere:

- The ecology of complex systems like river systems and wetlands versus private property rights of individuals
- The complex social causes of poverty versus a focus on individual initiative
- The complex health care system versus private accounts
- Our complex economy versus lower taxes for individuals

It is surely not the case that conservatives are simpleminded and cannot think in terms of complex systems: Indeed, conservative strategists consistently outdo progressive strategists when it comes to long-term, overall strategic initiatives. But when it comes to forming arguments based on moral or political reasoning, this difference seems to keep coming up.

TWO KINDS OF CAUSATION

Direct causation is the simplest kind: There is a single agent who purposely exerts force on something and as a result that thing moves or changes. You throw a ball and the ball goes through the air. You flip a light switch and the light turns on. The properties of direct causation are simple: One agent. One entity affected. One action, performed freely (using free will). No intermediate cause. No multiple agents.

What is at issue here is how the event is conceptualized, not the way it occurs in the world. Overthrowing a dictator may take millions of actions by hundreds of thousands of troops, but it can be conceptualized as a single action, carried out at the level of the army or the nation. "Bush overthrew Saddam Hussein" is an example of a complex phenomenon in the world being conceptualized as direct causation.

Systemic causation is rather different. Complex systems are commonplace. Examples are the stock market, weather systems, the power grid, the economy, a culture, the electorate, an ecosystem, an epidemic, the health care system, a social phenomenon (e.g., crime).

Systemic causation is a causal relation involving at least one complex system. Examples are very common: Global warming is causing the melting of the polar ice cap. The use of fossil fuels is causing global warming. The health care system is breaking down. The rise in health care costs is putting stress on the economy.

Notice the use of the present participle, "is causing, " "is putting stress," "is breaking down." A complex system functions over a significant amount of time, during which human preventive or corrective action can occur.

Moreover, complex systems are not easy to pin down to single events or event types. To get a hold on them, one has to use metaphoric or metonymic indicators—which do not exist as things in the world but give one a way of conceptualizing and measuring the state of some aspect of the world. Examples are stock market averages, average global temperature, health care cost indicators, the gross domestic product, and the number of diabetes patients treated in hospitals each year. To make causal statements with any rigor, one has to use statistical correlations among indicators and then impute causation to correlations. Since the indicators are, for the most part, not real things, and since correlation isn't causation, indicators and the correlations among them must be supplemented with a theory linking cause and the effect, for example a theory of how the use of fossil fuels leads to global warming or a theory of how health-care costs affect the economy.

Social, economic, and political policies are based on assumptions about causation. Consider the following progressive argument:

> The food industry has caused an increase in obesity, and, with it, the current diabetes epidemic, which threatens health-care costs, and food industry lobbying is stopping government regulation that could change the American diet and prevent future obesity and diabetes.

It contains the following complex systems: the food industry, obesity, the diabetes epidemic, health-care costs, and the (degree of healthiness of the) American diet. Since complex systems are widespread, they are not easily subject to control by individuals and so government action is seen as necessary.

Consider a response in a conservative vein:

> People get fat because they are undisciplined and eat too much, exercise too little, and eat the wrong foods. This is a matter of individual choice and individual responsibility. Everyone should be individually responsible for the

state of his health and his own health-care costs. That's why consumer-driven health insurance is both the fairest and most effective option. If you take care of yourself, your health-care costs will be less, and they should be. If your health care costs more, that is an incentive to eat better and lose weight.

This argument has no complex systems and no systemic causation. It is all a matter of individual discipline, individual action, and an individual weighting of costs and benefits. It ignores genetic factors both in obesity and in diabetes; specific genes have now been isolated that tend to make diabetes more likely (genetic effects are also systemic). It ignores the marketing of unhealthy foods as being causal. The fact that the food industry makes its money on that marketing—especially on marketing to children—indicates that marketing does have a causal effect. But since marketing is a complex system and its causal effect is not a matter of individual responsibility, it will tend not to be used in conservative arguments.

Now let us consider what these forms of causation have to do with freedom.

CAUSATION AND FREEDOM

Case 1. Simple freedom has the condition that you are free to act only if you do not impose on the freedom of others. Causing harm to others imposes on their freedom. Therefore you are free to act only if you do not cause harm to others. That is one of the logical connections between causation and freedom.

What is contested is what counts as causing harm. Does only direct causation count? Or does systemic causation count?

Suppose you own the mineral rights to a mountain in West

Virginia and you want to blow the top off it and start mining coal. Suppose you don't have the money for equipment and can get the money only by stealing it. Stealing money causes financial harm and is thus an imposition on the victim's freedom. According to simple freedom, you are not free to cause harm by stealing the money and then mining the coal. Stealing money is directly causing harm, and conservatives as well as progressives would recognize this as a prohibition.

Now suppose you have the mineral rights and the money for the equipment. You intend to blow off the top of the mountain and start mining coal, sending large amounts of pollution into nearby streams. That pollution would contain mercury, which poisons the water, poisons fish, builds up in the environment, and ultimately winds up in people's bodies, including the bodies of pregnant women. Right now, one woman out of six in America of childbearing age has so much mercury in her body that it threatens the viability of the fetus and can contribute to serious birth defects. Your coal mine would be contributing systemically to causing mercury poisoning, infant death, and lifelong illness. Should you be free to contribute systemically to causing such harm?

Progressives tend to say no, that such mining practices should be banned. They would argue on the basis of a significant contribution to the systemic causation of harm. And because the cause is systemic and widespread, only government action can be effective.

Conservatives tend to argue that your coal mine would not directly cause any known particular deaths or illness, and so you—and others—should be free to mine your coal. Government regulation would only get in the way of your legitimate right to do business and make a profit.

Case 2. Suppose you are brought up in a culture of poverty and ignorance. Are you free to take advantage of the educational and economic opportunities that America offers? Or might the culture you were brought up in be standing in your way, blocking such freedom?

Conservatives tend to argue that this is simply a matter of discipline and individual initiative. Here is Sean Hannity's version of the argument in *Let Freedom Ring*:

> That's the thing about freedom. It doesn't guarantee success . . . But let's say you show a little self-discipline—even if you haven't before . . . Let's say you go to bed at a reasonable hour at night and get up early in the morning to tackle the day. Let's say you really work hard. You develop marketable skills. You help invent or produce or distribute some product or service that people want or need. You get out and hustle. Rather than waste your money, you pay off your college loans and your credit cards and your car loans . . . You get serious about your life . . . and your sense of personal responsibility. What's going to happen? I guarantee you. You'll be on the road to success.

If you have the freedom to enter the free market, then educational and economic success are just a matter of discipline and individual initiative (direct causation).

Progressives tend to argue rather differently.

> If you are brought up in a culture of poverty and ignorance, you may not be raised to value learning and discursive arguments, to enjoy reading and other things done in school, and to function in a professional culture. Early cultural experience (a complex system) shapes your brain and thereby may place limits on your freedom to function well in school and in the business world.

It is not just a matter of discipline. Early cultural experience (a complex system) may systemically cause your brain to be shaped so that you cannot function in an educational or a professional environment. You may need early childhood education and other appropriate experiences.

Case 3. Suppose that we consider the group of, say, forty-five million working Americans (a complex system) who cannot afford health care (a complex system) because they are "unskilled" and cannot be paid much for their labor in this economy. Are all forty-five million jointly free to pull themselves up by their bootstraps in an economy structured to lower the cost of labor? Or is the structure of the economy a systemic cause limiting their freedom?

The progressive argument is that the economy does not have nearly enough well-paying jobs for those forty-five million people, and moreover, some forty-five million people would have to do the work these people now do for that low pay. Although some small number may be free to pull themselves up by their bootstraps, the structure of the economy (a complex system) is *a* systemic cause limiting the freedom of the whole group (a complex system).

The most likely conservative response is that in a group that large there will always be winners and losers, but those who are the most disciplined will be the winners who do pull themselves up by their bootstraps, and the losers will be those who are less disciplined and who therefore do not deserve to be winners. Individual initiative (direct causation) is the key.

Case 4. We know from our study of simple freedom that causing harm is imposing on one's freedom. We know also that freedom requires order and the rule of law. The question is this: Has George W. Bush brought freedom to the Iraqi people by waging the Iraq War?

The progressive answer is no. The war (a complex system) has resulted in the deaths of tens of thousands of Iraqis and the maiming of hundreds of thousands of others. It has brought devastation to much of the infrastructure of the country, it has resulted in an unemployment rate of about 50 percent, it has led to women being far less free than before, and it has brought civil chaos to much of the country. In each case, the causation of lessened freedom is systemic.

The conservative response would be something like this: Bush toppled Saddam Hussein (direct causation in the war frame), freeing Iraqis by direct action from his tyranny. Those killed and maimed don't count, since they are outside the war frame. Moreover, Bush has done nothing via direct causation to harm any Iraqis and so has not imposed on their freedom.

Let us now ask why progressives tend to focus on systemic causation and why conservatives focus on direct causation in their moral and political arguments.

CAUSATION IN THE FAMILY-BASED MODELS

Moral and political reasoning by conservatives and progressives uses the strict father and nurturant parent models. What is interesting about this is that the strict father model tends to use direct causation, while the nurturant parent model tends to use systemic causation. This difference can explain why progressives and conservatives think differently about causation and hence about freedom.

Think back to that part of the strict father model in which there is an absolute right and wrong, children are born bad in the sense that they just do what they want to do, and they have to be taught right from wrong. The father knows right from wrong and has the strength and authority to mete out rewards and punishments. That makes him a legitimate moral authority. In the model, the only way to teach a child morality is punishment for doing wrong, reward for doing right, and the assumption is that, to avoid punishment, the child will develop an internal discipline to do right and avoid wrong, which is the only way to teach morality. The child is told that the right thing is to obey, that he or she has the free will to obey or not, that he or she must develop the internal discipline to obey ("Just say no!"), and that direct punishment is the only way to provide the incentive for obedience.

The model requires a complex and deep set of assumptions about what a person is like and what morality is:

- A directive is a commandment, an order, a rule, or a clearly defined moral obligation with a clearly defined condition that would satisfy the directive.
- A person can understand a directive—and can understand what would count as obeying or disobeying that directive, and the necessary rewards and punishments.
- Moral behavior is obedience to the directives of a legitimate moral authority—a parent, God, a law, and ultimately oneself.
- A person has free will and can choose to obey or disobey a directive.
- In the typical case, obedience or disobedience is a single event with a single well-defined outcome by a single person caused directly via applying free will. If you are told to take out the garbage, you take it out or you don't.
- These are cases of direct causation.
- In the typical case, only such acts merit reward or punishment.
- There are certain major reasons for disobedience to the directive of a moral authority:
    1. Desire: the pull of the passions is stronger than the will to obey.
    2. Inability: the will to obey is there but cannot be carried out for reasons beyond one's control.

   3. Laziness: there is no desire to put the necessary
      energy into acting the right way.
   4. A challenge to authority: there is a will to disobey.
- Internal discipline is the proper response to all four
  cases.
      1. Discipline involves strengthening the will to
         overrule the passions.
      2. Discipline requires gaining control over external
         factors. There are no excuses.
      3. Discipline involves gathering the necessary energy
         and using it.
      4. Discipline involves bending one's own will to the
         will of another.
- Character is defined by using discipline and free will to
  follow the directives of one's internalized legitimate
  moral authority.
- The purpose of reward and punishment by the strict father is to develop character in a child by the time the
  child reaches adulthood.

I want to call attention to the direct causation in the typical
case. Moral action is learned as freely willed single actions by a
single individual that directly result in a clearly defined outcome.
Strict father morality makes one tend to pay special attention to
direct causation over and over throughout one's upbringing and
beyond.

The nurturant parent model, on the other hand, tends to pay
attention to systemic causation. Empathy and responsibility have
their effects over a period of time and a range of situations. Children learn positive attachment via regular complex interaction
with a parent, in which they observe and mimic empathic and
responsible behavior.

A nurturant community ("It takes a village"), where groups
of people cooperate to serve the community, plays an important
role in moral development. The actions of the whole population

(a complex system) have an overall systemic causal effect on the moral formation of the child.

Morality is not just obeying particular directives. Morality inheres in systemic causation, judging via long and wide experience what makes things better for people and acting accordingly overall.

Discipline is required not just to act responsibly in cases of one-on-one interaction or individual initiative (direct causation) but also to learn to notice in a systematic way what tends to help or harm others.

Character is the ability to discern through empathy how to operate in a complex social system so as to help and avoid acting in ways that harm.

Moral directives of course exist, because certain moral situations tend to recur: Be protective, be fair, be respectful, use your talents, be joyful (so as to be more empathetic), be cooperative, be honest and trustworthy, be open.

But the focus is not on direct rewards and punishments for individual acts. Good and bad things happen to you depending on your ability to function nurturantly in your community. Your feedback is complex and part of a system. And you learn to notice complex systemic causality.

This difference shows up as a moral and political difference. Conservative moral philosophy makes individual responsibility uppermost, while progressive thought centers on social and ecological, as well as individual responsibility.

SYSTEMIC CAUSATION
AND THE ENVIRONMENT

Every ecosystem is a complex system governed by systemic causation. Old-growth forests, for example, are enormously complex ecological systems—not just habitats for owls. Their value is, in part, spiritual: Each old-growth forest is a wondrously complex ecology of supreme value in itself that reflects the magnificent complexity that governed our evolution.

The issue is not just saving owls. Owls are symbolic. They eat rodents. They live in trees. Dead trees decay into nutrients for the soil, which gives life to other plants, which feed songbirds and other animals.

Such forests help define our identity—our animal nature. They tell us what it means to have co-evolved as animals with a huge variety of plants and other animals. The fact that it is a complex system governed by complex causation is part of its inherent value. It is part of environmental freedom—the freedom to connect with, commune with, and enjoy nature.

Strict father morality comes with the idea of the moral order, with man over nature, people over animals and plants—with the idea that nature is there purely for profit, to be exploited, not preserved. That is why conservatives frame the issue as owls versus people. The conservative frame of the moral order gives the answer: People are more important than owls. Trees are there for our profit.

Profit, moreover, is taken in the narrow sense of direct causation: cut down the trees (direct causation), sell them (direct causation), and do it efficiently by clear-cutting to maximize profit—for logging corporations, their management, owners, and investors.

But when systemic causation is brought into play, our understanding of profit changes. Forests prevent flooding, which destroys homes. Natural beauty brings tourists, who spend money on local businesses. The wealthy prefer vacation homes in and near forests, and they too spend money there on local businesses. That raises property values. Living and working near forests is healthy and enjoyable. "Profit" from forests need not mean just cutting down trees for corporations to sell.

Conservatives tend to approach ecological issues in terms of direct causation—short-term jobs lost, profits lost. For what? A few owls. Progressives tend to look at ecological issues in terms of systemic causation over a long history and an indefinite future. Cost-benefit analysis uses direct causation implicitly. Do a calculation over a reasonably compact circumscribed region, a short-term starting and ending point, with only certain measurable things entering the calculation, with the values translated into monetary terms and based on the short-term corporate profits and costs. It's all direct causal thinking, not the systemic thinking required by ecological issues.

Conservative ideology questions the significance of global warming and even questions its existence. Global warming is the granddaddy of all systemic causation issues. Without a grasp of systemic causation, it cannot be comprehended at all. It is not surprising that it is conservatives, not progressives, who are in denial over the existence of global warming.

CAUSATION, IDEOLOGY, AND PUBLIC POLICY

Hurricane Katrina is a perfect illustration of systemic causation and the freedom issues that arise from it.

We know that the strength of a hurricane depends on the amount of heating over the surface of water. As a result of global warming, the heating of the gulf waters has been rising steadily over the past few decades. The rise in 2005 indicated, via statistical correlation, that the heat of the gulf would produce an extraordinary number of class-four and class-five hurricanes. A certain percentage of those hurricanes head toward New Orleans. With more and more violent hurricanes in 2005, the odds were high that a class-four or -five storm would hit New Orleans. The warning came well in advance. But it was complex and systematic, not a direct prediction of a specific storm with a particular force on a particular date.

The issue was moral and political action. The Bush administration ignored the warnings. Increases in the odds of a class-four or -five hurricane hitting New Orleans had been predicted for years. Hurricane experts noted that the levees needed repair. Funds were allocated—and then cut by the Bush administration and designated instead for two directly caused acts: the Iraq War and a specific tax cut, mostly going to the wealthiest Americans. Political ideology, under the cognitive governance of strict father morality, ruled the day. Direct causation won out over systemic causation.

The right-wing attack on science is not an attack on all science. The sciences attacked are those that rely the most on systemic causation: evolution and global warming. There is no attack on Newtonian physics—no attack on billiard ball causation, conservation of momentum, conservation of energy, or even gravity (you drop something, it falls).

CAUSATION AND TORTURE

I wondered for many years how conservatives got away over and over with the bad apple defense. Take Abu Ghraib. We know that the people who carried out the torture at Abu Ghraib, Guantánamo, and elsewhere were working from guidelines prepared by higher-ups, perhaps even at the level of the secretary of defense. Investigations have shown the systematic involvement of people in the military high command. Yet only some of the people actually doing the torturing have been tried and punished. The higher-ups have gone scot-free, on the bad apple defense: It was just some lower-level bad apples that caused the trouble. Why?

The people prosecuted and punished were only those in-volved in unitary direct torture. They were not people in a sys-tem of torture policy, all of whom played a causal role. Systemic torture policy is pooh-poohed and ignored by conservatives. It seems not to fit their system of thought.

CAUSATION AND SIN

The distinction between systemic causality and freely willed di-rect causality occurs repeatedly in many disputes.

- My wood burning isn't responsible for the woodsmoke pollution in my city.
- The water taken from the river for my farm won't kill off all the fish in the river.
- The old-growth redwood I am buying for my deck won't kill off the old-growth redwood forests.
- My smoking won't give you cancer.

In each case, the problem is systemic causation to which every-one contributes a little freely willed direct causal action that, in itself, has no noticeable effect; but the little causes in a system add up to a huge cause.

Conservative populism, as discussed in Chapter 8, makes par-tial use of direct causal reasoning, pooh-poohing the progressives who are reasoning systemically and empathetically in terms of how the freedom of others is violated through systemic causa-tion. Should you feel guilty for your small direct act that, in it-self, adds up to little? A sin, in the typical case, is disobedience to a clear moral directive performed in a freely willed single di-rect act. A sin is something you have individual responsibility for. Where there is massive systemic causation that you contribute a tiny unnoticeable part to, is that a sin? Not from a strict father perspective. That's one of the reasons that conservatives talk about "environmental wackos." They tend not to count small systemic contributions as sins or immoral acts because there are no discernible consequences of the single freely willed direct act.

A typical example is the "What would Jesus drive?" campaign against SUVs. Here is the text of a progressive Christian anti-SUV ad from the January 2003 edition of *Christianity Today*:

> To some, the question might seem amusing. But we take it seriously. As our Savior and Lord Jesus Christ teaches us, "Love your neighbor as yourself" (Mark 12:30–31).
>
> Of all the choices we make as consumers, the cars we drive have the biggest impact on all of God's creation. Car pollution causes illness and death, and most afflicts the elderly, poor, sick and young. It also contributes to global warming, putting millions at risk from drought, flood, hunger and homelessness.
>
> Transportation is now a moral choice and an issue for Christian reflection. It's about more than engineering— it's about ethics. About obedience. About loving our neighbor.
>
> *So what would Jesus drive?* We call upon America's automobile industry to manufacture more fuel-efficient vehicles. And we call upon Christians to drive them.
>
> Because it's about more than vehicles—it's about values.

This ad campaign originated with the Evangelical Environmental Network, publishers of *Creation Care* magazine. EEN is concerned with getting progressive Christians to understand the moral imperative of environmental issues—saving God's creation, cleaning up pollution, and preserving the environment.

One of their challenges is getting evangelical Christians to comprehend systemic causation and that it involves individual choices, which hence are matters of individual moral responsibility. Though the ad is overtly about SUVs, the issue is symbolic, intended to raise the general issue of individual responsibility for care for the environment.

Specifically, the ad raises the religious question of whether you are morally free to pollute, or whether pollution, by causing harm, impinges on the freedom of others, and hence you are not morally free to pollute. Is your small freely willed contribution to systemic pollution a sin?

The right-wing fundamentalist responses make fun of the very idea that contributing to pollution could count as a sin. If you want to get into heaven, you should avoid the real sins, things the Bible says not to do, the freely willed directly causal acts. Polluting doesn't count as sin because, first, it is not a direct sinful act, and second, because pollution is the natural state of the earth since the Fall and you shouldn't expect it to be pure.

Here is Terry Watkins of Dial-the-Truth Ministries:

This world is polluted.

And it's polluted bad. Very, very, bad . . .

The REAL pollution took place 6,000 years ago in the garden of Eden. When Adam and Eve rebelled against the will of God and ate the forbidden fruit—this pure, clean, sinless, earth became polluted, cursed and dirty. This earth is a cursed, polluted, corrupt environment because of the rebellion of man . . .

But God loves you SO much . . . More than you can even begin to conceive. He loved you SO much that He gave His only begotten Son to remove and cleanse the pollution of your sin. Jesus Christ came into this world to die on a cross, shed His precious, sinless, pure, unpolluted blood for you.

Another response showing that contributing to pollution isn't taken as sin is belittlement via punning. Here is Terry Watkins again:

> In Jeremiah the Lord drives the children of Israel in His Plymouth Fury:
>
> Behold, I will gather them out of all countries, **whither I have driven them . . . in my fury** . . . (Jeremiah 32:27).

The fundamentalist response makes a joke out of the very idea.

The libertarian response is interesting in another way. It reframes the question in terms of the market and consumer choice. Here is William L. Anderson of *The Free Market*, the Mises Institute monthly:

> they want the government to make sure you cannot spend your money where you would like, at least when it comes to purchasing automobiles . . . we are willing to trade some gasoline mileage for the safety and comfort that the vans provide. I do not think our choice was between sin and righteousness, but rather between one set of costs and another.

Framing the choice in terms of the market removes moral responsibility. The market is seen, via metaphor, as both natural and moral—moral because the invisible hand (its natural mechanism) guarantees that it will maximize benefit for all. Operating within the market is therefore not harmful to anyone and cannot interfere with the freedom of others. This is free-market freedom at work. The act of choosing could not have been a sin simply because it is in the market—a market-based choice, not a direct violation of a biblical commandment. In the market, the issue of sin is moot—you cannot sin by buying an SUV.

What is particularly interesting here is that the market is a causal system—an extremely complex system where it is difficult to determine the effect of any one choice. It inherently involves systemic causation. But the metaphor of the market—if each person seeks his own profit (direct causation), then the profit of all will be maximized (by the invisible hand)—turns a complex system via metaphor into a system governed by individual direct causation. Even the metaphor of a single invisible hand having the causal effect is a case of direct causation.

You can see why the "What would Jesus drive?" campaign never caught on with conservative Christians.

Many questions of freedom come down to questions of causation—systemic or direct. Because of the details of the strict father versus nurturant parent models, radical conservatives and progressives tend to see causality—and with it, morality—in very different ways. Moral responsibility is, of course, about freedom, about the question of what you are morally free to do. Differences in perceptions of causation have everything to do with differences in judgments about freedom and hence about what is moral.

Suppose it is true that those using strict father morality tend to favor direct causation in moral decisions and largely ignore systemic causality, while those with nurturant parent morality readily admit systemic causality into moral decisions. What follows is a major split in our understanding of what is real—a split along moral and political lines!

It is hard to overestimate how important this is. Our understanding of causation defines what we take to be real in the world and what we take to be the consequences of our actions. Political decisions affect reality. What is disturbing is that political ideology can so deeply affect the understanding of what is real and so thoroughly hide the real consequences of so many political decisions.

I should point out, in conclusion, that the argument in this chapter—and in this book as a whole—is based on systemic causation. Conceptual systems are systems, after all. There are systems of conservative and progressive thought, and I am endeavoring to describe their causal effects. The irony, in this case, is that I am using systemic causation to study the difference between systemic and direct causation. It makes me wonder whether such a book could be written only by a progressive.

PART III

FORMS OF FREEDOM

8

PERSONAL FREEDOM AND POPULISM

In political speeches, freedom is often spoken of in grand terms: self-government, free elections, freedom of speech and religion—the great ideas of American democracy. What is lost in this rhetoric are the nitty-gritty personal freedoms of everyday life, often unnoticed until they are gone.

Liberals and conservatives have very different ideas of what constitutes nitty-gritty personal freedom. Indeed, in many cases what are freedoms for liberals contradicts what counts as freedom for conservatives. Understanding this difference is politically important, since it lies behind much of conservative populism—the idea that ordinary working people are under attack by a liberal elite and that conservatives represent the values of ordinary folks. This flies in the face of the liberal idea that liberals are the true populists, defending the material interests of the working poor and the middle class. Socioeconomic liberals wonder why poor and middle-class conservatives vote against their material self-interest; they recommend a populist electoral strategy without understanding conservative populism and the role that the conservative notion of personal freedom plays in it.

Conservatives have a litany of lost freedoms, a litany that serves as a call to arms against the "liberal elite," the snobs who, according to conservative orthodoxy, look down their noses at ordinary Americans trying to exercise their God-given freedoms. In the culture wars, the liberal attitude is called "political correctness," a snide term suggesting that liberals think they know what's right and are trying to impose it politically on ordinary people, who know better.

WHAT IS CONSERVATIVE POPULISM?

So far as I have been able to tell, conservative populism has several factors. The first is the ordinary people frame, in which there is a contrast between the elite and the ordinary people. In this frame, the ordinary people are the good people and the elite are their oppressors. The elite are snobs who look down on the ordinary people, and especially look down on their values. Snobbishness can have many parameters: wealth, education, body image, language, social position, body language, and taste in clothes, food, forms of recreation, consumer goods, places to shop.

Populism is about identifying oneself as an ordinary person, oppressed by the elite. The ordinary person is poor, uneducated, hardworking (doing manual labor), physically strong, religious, patriotic, uses bad grammar, has loosely articulated pronunciation, and has a traditional sex role.

Men fit certain stereotypes: in the South, good ol' boys; in the Midwest, farmboys; in the West, cowboys. The word "boy" is not accidental here. There is a notion that "boys will be boys," that a certain male naughtiness is part of the stereotype.

Marketers have picked up on the stereotype. Music: country western. Recreation: Nascar races, football, gambling. Drink: workingman's beer, namely, Bud, Miller, Coors. Car: SUV. Dress: jeans. Food: fast food, meat. Religion: fundamentalism. Shoes: boots (preferably cowboy boots).

Conservative populism takes advantage of this stereotype and brands liberals: limousine liberals, Hollywood liberals, Volvo-driving Birkenstock-wearing latte-sipping sushi-eating liberals.

Conservatives have politicized populism. Conservatism iden-tifies the ordinary person as an ordinary American, a conserva-tive patriot with conservative values (strict father morality). And they have identified the elite as the liberal elite, with lib-eral political and social values: feminism, gay rights, environ-mentalism, peace, protection, safety, anti–death penalty, high culture. Liberals are portrayed not just as effete social snobs, but as political snobs who tell people what to believe about politics—what is politically correct or PC.

Conservative populism is significantly about freedom. Part of liberal oppression is the intrusion of liberal PC values on per-sonal conservative freedoms.

LIBERTY

The word "liberty" tends to be used more by conservatives than by progressives. And the conservatives who use it tend to be populists. This entry in the Mac dictionary explains why: "Lib-erty" is the state of being free within society from oppressive re-strictions imposed by authority on one's way of life, behavior, or political views.

"Liberty" may, like "freedom," refer to the state of being free. But "liberty" comes with a very different frame than "freedom."

Here is what the liberty frame looks like:

- There are within society oppressive restrictions im-posed by authority on one's way of life, behavior, or po-litical views.
- Liberty is *freedom from* those oppressive restrictions.
- Liberty is also *freedom to* do positive things you feel you

have the right to be free to do given your way of life, or the way of life you think you should have.

To a conservative populist, the oppressive restrictions are called political correctness. They are seen as imposed by a liberal elite. Conservative populists resent that elite.

Exactly what is oppressive to a conservative populist, and why? So far as I can tell, the following are the sources of such oppression:

- Their way of life is governed by strict father morality, which can determine what positive things they feel they have a right to do.
- The oppressive restrictions arise from the condition that one is not free to interfere with the freedom of others. The question is, What counts as interfering with the freedom of others?
- Suppose that "interference" either involves systemic causality, which they do not recognize as valid, or assumes nurturant morality, which they reject. Any such restriction against interference will not be seen as valid.
- The everyday things they feel they should have a right to do are being blocked by either a liberal view of morality or a liberal understanding of systemic causation. That feels like oppression by uppity liberals who think they know what's right and how ordinary folks should live.
- Liberals who speak of such interference are seen as either crazies, extremists, elites who don't know how real people live, or uncaring authoritarians.

Conservative Christians often speak of "religious liberty"— what they see as the political freedom to practice their religion as they choose to. That practice includes spreading the "good news," the truth of Gospel. They do not see this as an imposition on the freedom of others, since they are helping others by communicating to them how to avoid the torture of hell and achieve the bliss of heaven. Displaying the Ten Commandments in schools and courts is seen as offering freedom from hell, not imposing on freedom. School prayer is a perfect example of direct action: one child saying one prayer on one occasion. Saying a prayer, or reading a passage from the Christian Bible, is simple and natural in that way of life. To see school prayer as a harmful act requires, first, empathy with non-Christians and atheists— sinners who are going to hell—and second, the effects of peer pressure and fears of in-group exclusion, which are complex.

Other conservatives speak of owning and using guns in terms of liberty, of freedom from taxation as a liberty issue, and of liberty being at stake in restrictions on suburban and exurban development.

The word "liberty" tends to be used more by conservatives than by progressives because it focuses on individual freedom of choice and not on the imposition of that choice on others. And it tends to be used more by, and for audiences of, conservative populists, who see themselves as culturally oppressed by values they don't believe in or views of causation that make no sense to them.

Progressives, because of empathy and their sense of systemic causality, pay particular attention to how everyday acts can impose on the freedom of others: how driving SUVs can dirty the air and contribute to global warming; how secondhand smoke can be harmful to nonsmokers; how taking water from a river can kill the fish and other aquatic life; how dams can lead to salmon extinction; how hate speech both reflects and reinforces hate, and contributes to violence; how Wal-Mart's low prices lead to low pay, no benefits, higher taxes, and the destruction of communities; how cutting down old-growth forests eliminates habitats for species. Conservative populists often see these acts either as imposing on their values, or as not making any sense.

POPULISM AND IDENTITY

Conservative populism is also about identity as an ordinary American. The main areas of identity are family, religion, community, love of the land, forms of recreation, work, and health.

Here are some examples of conservative freedoms—or liberties—that conservative populists claim are either under attack or already taken away and need to be reclaimed.

- The freedom to decide what is going to be taught to my children—what is taught about history, science, sex, religion, and morality—should fit my values.
- The freedom to use or dispose of my property as I see fit—without government intervening with antisprawl laws, or zoning, or environmental regulations.
- The freedom to get rid of waste in the easiest and cheapest way—burning leaves, dumping waste in streams, burying garbage in the earth or the ocean.
- The freedom to have a wood fire in my fireplace—regardless of its contribution to local pollution.
- The freedom to defend myself and my family with any kind of gun I decide I need—even automatic weapons.
- The freedom to hunt—regardless of whether I am hunting an endangered species.
- The freedom to use any kind of vehicle anywhere—an SUV to drive over rough terrain, a snowmobile in Yellowstone, a dune buggy in the desert, a speedboat on a lake—without having to worry about sensitive habitats or other people's sensibilities.

- The freedom to extract and use any natural resource to make a living—without having to care about environmental effects.
- The freedom to take water from a river to irrigate my farm—regardless of its consequences for fish or other aquatic life in the river.
- The freedom to make as much money as I can, as long as it is legal.
- The freedom to hire or promote or fire anyone I please—without having to worry about discriminatory hiring or labor policies.
- The freedom to offer any wage to an employee—without having to worry about unions, minimum wage laws, working conditions, or medical benefits.
- The freedom to make and sell any kind of product— free of governmental agencies judging whether it is safe or effective.
- The freedom to grow and sell any kind of food—without having to worry about pesticide use or food safety regulations.
- The freedom to build and develop anywhere—wetlands, sensitive habitats, beaches, riverbanks, floodplains.
- The freedom to say anything to anybody—even if the language is degrading or hurtful.
- The freedom to practice and promulgate my religion— even in public, using public facilities.
- The freedom to do business without the threat of class action lawsuits.
- The freedom to choose among the widest range of consumer products possible at the lowest possible prices— without having to worry about third-world sweatshops, employee working conditions, effects on small businesses, old-growth forests, pollution, monocultures.

- The freedom to decide how I spend the money I earn.
- The freedom to live in a community without threats to myself or my family from immoral people—drug addicts, ex-convicts, sexual predators, pornographers, gays.
- The freedom to live in a country and a community with values I identify with—values that do not threaten my sense of who I am, what I should be, or how I should bring up my children.

To ideological conservatives, these are fundamental freedoms, and the threat or loss of them constitutes tyranny, a threat to America's defining ideal—liberty—a threat so visceral it threatens their very identity and way of life. This threat is what fuels the culture wars and defines conservative populism.

What makes these conservative views of freedom? And what makes these freedoms to conservatives?

The answer is strict father morality, as contrasted with nurturant morality. Strict father morality says that every moral adult has incorporated the right values and the right discipline, which has earned him or her the freedom to be his or her own moral authority. The natural and moral mechanism for this freedom is, as I have explained, the unconstrained free market, in which the free pursuit of individual self-interest maximizes the self-interest of everyone and thus best serves the community and the country.

Conservative freedom is the ultimate in freedom to and freedom from for each person, individually. It maximizes individual initiative and individual responsibility. Strict morality contrasts with nurturant morality, which you'll recall focuses on individual responsibility (taking care of yourself) and social responsibility (caring about and working actively for the freedom of others).

Each of the above forms of freedom fits strict morality and violates nurturant morality. The violations occur in the area of empathy, the responsibility to act on that empathy, the recognition of systemic causation, and the social necessity to build a shared infrastructure that is necessary for the achievement of individual goals.

For example, many of the conservative freedoms—say, unlimited property rights or unconstrained business practices—can adversely affect other people, thus interfering with other people's freedoms. Under nurturant morality, that interference with the freedom of others disqualifies the practice as a freedom; it need not under strict father morality, if the interference doesn't count as interference under strict father morality, or if the causation involved is systemic, not direct.

A PROGRESSIVE POPULISM

Conservative populism is based on strict father morality, its role in personal and cultural identity, and the way it extends simple freedom to the conservative version of freedom. The conservative message machine has created conservative populism by branding liberalism as an oppressor and conservative values as patriotic. The result has been to forge a conservative populist identity, within a moral and cultural war of conservative liberty versus oppression by the liberal elite.

Just as conservatives are more aware of, and able to articulate, their moral values, so they are more aware of the freedoms implied by those values. Progressives are less aware of, and less able to articulate, their implicit (real and felt) moral values and so are less aware of the concept of freedom that implicitly follows from those values but is rarely explicitly discussed. Progressives have a sense that conservatives are in the process of taking their freedoms, but those freedoms must be articulated if they are to be preserved and expanded. Here are progressive freedoms that are now being threatened or have been lost:

- The freedom to be told the truth by my government: freedom of open information.
- The freedom to have my children taught the truth and taught about the diversity of values in our culture and other cultures.
- The freedom to find a good job and make a decent living at it through work.
- The freedom to use or dispose of my property so as not to interfere with the freedom of others, and the freedom from the harmful use or disposal of property by others.
- Freedom from pollution by others.
- Freedom from the threat of those possessing and able to use deadly weapons, except for those exercising legitimate police powers.
- The freedom to connect with the physical environment and the living things in it, and to see both preserved so that my progeny and progeny of others can do so as well.
- The freedom to explore our common natural heritage without harming it.
- The freedom to enjoy the preservation of our waterways and oceans and the aquatic life therein.
- The freedom to live in a country free from discrimination and committed to reversing the harmful effects of past discrimination.
- The freedom to buy safe products—guaranteed through regulation.
- The freedom to eat safe food—food that is pesticide free, hormone free, antibiotic free, free of genetically modified ingredients, healthy, and uncontaminated.
- The freedom to speak freely without harming anyone by the use of degrading or hurtful language and without being so harmed.

- The freedom to practice my religion, if I have one, privately, without imposing it on the public or using public resources to support or promulgate it, and without having any other person's religion imposed on me.
- The freedom to do business freely and ethically—with the public protected through both government regulation and the civil justice system.
- The freedom to choose among the widest range of consumer products possible at the lowest possible prices produced by ethical businesses—businesses that avoid third-world sweatshops, child labor, detrimental working conditions, detrimental effects on small businesses, preserve old-growth forests, minimize pollution, do not impose monocultures.
- The freedom to make use of the common infrastructure provided by the use of the common wealth for the common good—highways and other physical infrastructure, public schools, communication systems, public health systems, disaster relief systems, the banking system, the courts.
- The freedom to live in a community where my family and I are as secure as possible and where everyone is treated fairly and humanely.
- The freedom to a private life not only free from government interference but also where government actively protects privacy—of personal information, of communication, of personal and family medical decisions, of sex lives, of personal associations.
- The freedom to live in a corruption-free political system minimally affected by concentrations of wealth.
- The freedom to live in a balanced economic system where assets do not unduly accrue to the wealthy and where there is no transfer of wealth from the general populace to the wealthy.

- The freedom of access to information through media minimally affected by concentrations of wealth and political power.
- Freedom from corporations exercising governing powers over one's private life with no accountability— HMOs making fateful decisions about permitted medical treatments, insurance companies determining whether you can be insured, auto companies deciding how much gas you will have to use, food companies deciding how healthy your foods will be, credit card companies deciding what you will pay to borrow money.
- The freedom to live in a country and a community governed by the traditional progressive values of empathy and responsibility—where leaders care about people and act responsibly toward them and where citizens care about each other and act responsibly toward each other and toward their country and their community.

These freedoms are consistent with progressive values—traditional American values. They are the freedoms we ought to have. Some of them have been taken away. Some are being taken away. In other cases, America has made progress toward them and the progress has been, or is being, reversed. Still other freedoms are implicit in our values but as yet unrealized.

Some of these are discussed widely, such as freedom from discrimination, from the effects of wealth on elections, from government intrusions into privacy. But the generalization is rarely made: These are all progressive freedoms. They all come from the same source, the traditional progressive values of empathy and responsibility. These are the values that lie behind our Constitution and our principal founding documents. And it has been the expanding realization of the freedoms defined by these values that we are most proud of.

Moreover, these are the freedoms that should underlie a truly progressive populism, not merely an economic populism. Populism is about identity—identity as an ordinary American, not just economic self-interest. One of the major components of identity is one's value system: strict, nurturant, or biconceptual (strict in some areas, nurturant in others). Conservatives have swung a preponderance of biconceptuals to their side by repeating conservative values—including conservative ideas of freedom—over and over on issue after issue, while putting down progressive values. But biconceptuals have progressive values as well as conservative ones. Progressives can appeal to biconceptuals through communicating progressive values and progressive ideas of freedom—conveyed honestly, assertively, and repeatedly, while criticizing conservative values, either explicitly or implicitly.

The key to appealing to biconceptuals is understanding which nurturant values are identity defining. Here are some of the key forms of identity that embody nurturant values:

- *Identification with the land*: either through its beauty, a sense of place, the way one makes a living (farming, ranching), or recreation (hunting, fishing, hiking, camping). Protection of the land can be seen as protection of the self; a threat to the land can be seen as a threat to the self. Freedom is the freedom to continue enjoying or using the land.
- *Identification with one's community*: Biconceptuals seem to prefer nurturant communities, with leaders who care about the citizens and are responsible to them, and where citizens care about each other and are responsible to each other and to the community as a whole. A threat to the community is a threat to the self; community improvement is self-improvement. Freedom is the freedom to live in and serve such a community.
- *Identification with one's religion*: Most Christians are pro-

gressive Christians, seeing God as a nurturant parent offering unconditional love, grace (metaphorical nurturance), understanding, forgiveness, and protection, and Christ as a model of caring about others and acting responsibly on that care (healing the sick, feeding the hungry, protecting the oppressed, uplifting the downtrodden, serving the poor). Freedom is freedom from the burden of sin, attained through good works (which earn restitution and forgiveness). Progressive Christians reject the idea of God as a punitive strict father, commanding obedience, demanding discipline, severely punishing, and threatening hell. Biconceptual Christians can be appealed to through their progressive side.

- *Identification with one's family*: Many biconceptuals are nurturant parents in the home and identify with their role as parents. They may be strict only in some other aspects of life. Freedom is spending time with, and caring for, your family.

- *Identification with one's job*: There are many biconceptuals whose jobs are inherently nurturant and who identify with those jobs: teachers, healers, caregivers, providers of social services, public advocates, and many, many more. Freedom is the ability to effectively help others.

- *Identification with one's person*: It is common to identify primarily with your very body: with your physical security, your health, your looks, your concerns about aging. Many biconceptuals see this concern as addressed through living in a culture of care and mutual responsibility, rather than a culture where you're on your own. In short, they identify with nurturant values when thinking of their bodies, though they may have strict values about other matters. Freedom is security and health.

- *Identification with one's country*: At election time and in times of crisis, it is common to identify with one's country and one's vision of how it should be. For some, one's identification as a patriot, as an American first and foremost, is one's primary identification. Many biconceptuals see progressive values as those defining America—the values of tolerance, equality, unity, opportunity, human dignity, mutual responsibility, and care for all. Freedom is mutual responsibility.

Populism depends on these forms of identification and the kinds of everyday freedoms associated with them. A progressive populism will require progressives and biconceptuals in the poor and middle classes to overwhelmingly adopt these forms of identity. Identification with one's own material well-being is secondary!

A progressive populism will also have to see ordinary Americans as progressives, and conservatives as a threatening elite—not merely wealthy and/or powerful, but as having values that represent a visceral threat to morality, identity, and patriotism: a threat to preserving the land, strengthening nurturant communities, living progressive religious values, supporting nurturant family life, making a living helping others and the community in general, finding security, identifying with one's country, devoting oneself to traditional progressive values.

Correspondingly, conservative populism wins when it succeeds in framing ordinary Americans as oppressed by a liberal elite. It wins when it identifies conservatism with patriotism. And it wins when strict father values dominate personal and cultural identification with the land, community, religion, family, kind of work, one's physical person, and one's country—and when nurturant values threaten those forms of identity.

Conservative populism has been carefully constructed and groomed for nearly forty years. It has been grounded in a preexisting conservative cultural populism in the South, Midwest, and

West. It is social and cultural at its root, and has had conservative political populism placed on top of it. A progressive populism must start with preexisting progressive social and cultural nurturant forms of identity. They exist, both in progressives and in biconceptuals.

But because conservative populism is already in place, progressive populists face an extraordinary challenge. They must activate progressive populism and destroy conservative populism at the same time. This is not an easy job.

Democrats—especially Al Gore and John Edwards—have tried to construct a progressive populism around economic issues alone. They failed and we can see why. They didn't take into account identity and culture. They didn't take into account strict father morality. They didn't take into account the liberal elite social stereotype and the liberal elite political PC stereotype. And they didn't take into account the role of personal freedom and systemic causation.

9

ECONOMIC FREEDOM

Let us begin with the obvious: Money has a lot to do with freedom. Wealth can provide freedom from want—from hunger, homelessness, many illnesses and dangers. It can buy access to education and health care. It can buy houses and cars. It can buy political influence. It can allow you to live where you want and how you want, within limits. Correspondingly, a lack of money can impinge mightily on your freedom.

Conservatives who speak of economic freedom are usually concerned with making and keeping money—that is, with the freedom to acquire and maintain further freedoms (the ones that money can buy). The government is, in Grover Norquist's term, "the beast"—to be shrunk to be small enough to drown in a bathtub. Their gripe against government is that government takes away their money (through taxes), gives it to other people (through social programs), gets in the way of making it (through regulations and laws), and wastes it (through inefficiency). In doing so, they see government as taking away not only their freedom but also their freedom to acquire and maintain other freedoms. They also believe that private wealth creates more wealth through investment and that government taxation and regulation inhibits the creation of more wealth and thus more freedom. The only legitimate role for government is to protect their freedom—their lives and property (the military, the police, and the criminal justice system)—and to provide order in their everyday lives (through law enforcement and institutions that promote social order, like churches).

Strict morality gives shape and provides moral fervor to such views. Since the discipline to be moral provides the discipline to be prosperous, only those with sufficient moral discipline deserve prosperity. Conservatives assume that the free market is the natural mechanism linking discipline to prosperity, that it allows everyone who is sufficiently disciplined to pull himself or herself up by the bootstraps. Those who haven't just aren't disciplined enough and don't deserve anything they don't earn.

Progressives, because empathy animates their worldview, tend to be concerned about those who don't have enough money—the hungry, the homeless, the impoverished, those without good jobs, or education, or skills. Because of their sense of responsibility, progressives want to help. They see it as the responsibility of the government to create programs to help those in need, to create good jobs, to increase wages for jobs that exist, and to provide education and health care. They understand the importance of the common wealth, that a shared infrastructure, built by redistributing resources, is essential to the individual pursuit of prosperity.

Conservatives counter that such programs don't help, they hurt. Giving people things they haven't earned takes away their incentive to be disciplined and hence makes them dependent and less capable of acting morally. The best way to create jobs, they counter, is to cut taxes for the wealthy and for corporations, thus giving them more money to spend and to invest in businesses that create jobs. Another way is to eliminate government regulation, consumer lawsuits, unions, and pensions that get in the way of corporations making profits—and hence being able to create more jobs.

Progressives counter that the wealthy tend to keep their money or invest abroad, and that the jobs created aren't good jobs with good pay and benefits, that they aren't jobs that expand freedom.

At present, conservatives have been dominating the public discourse and winning enough elections to control the strings of government.

Conservatives have gotten their economic ideas more and more into the public mind and into the workings of public policy. They have succeeded through their vast network of think tanks and their message machine of thousands of conservative media outlets, as well as training institutions, media agents, and spokespeople. Through all this, conservatives have propagated what I call the "economic liberty myth."

The myth takes for granted an important metaphor: Corporations are persons. This legal metaphor assigns to corporations many of the rights and responsibilities of persons—the right of free speech, the responsibility to pay taxes, the ability to sue and be sued in a civil suit. This metaphor places corporations firmly in the private, not the public, sphere.

In the economic liberty myth, corporations, via the corporations are persons metaphor, are seen as deserving of freedom and liberty, and subject, like people, to the oppression of government—rather than being part of the oppression of government. Adherents of the economic liberty myth talk about individual initiative, responsibility, and freedom, but their policies apply overwhelmingly less to individual people than to individual corporations and the people who own and run them.

THE ECONOMIC LIBERTY MYTH: THE RIGHT WING ECONOMIC FREEDOM STORY

Mythology matters. Myths reside in our brains, defining heroes and villains, moral and immoral actions, and what makes sense. Here is the myth that governs conservative economic thought:

- It's individual initiative, individual responsibility, and individual freedom that have made America great.
- Economic freedom is free access to and free participation in free markets.
- Free markets are both natural and moral: If everyone pursues his or her own profit, the profit of all will be maximized as a law of nature. (The reason is simple: Free markets are competitive, and competition maximizes efficiency, minimizes waste, minimizes costs, and maximizes benefits for all.)
- The free market is the natural mechanism of a thriving economy, and it works best without constraints that interfere with its operation—those imposed by taxes, government regulation, consumer lawsuits, unions, and corporate benefits.
- Government is the problem; it gets in the way of free markets and wastes taxpayers' money.
- Private industry is more efficient and less wasteful than government. As much of the government as possible should be privatized.
- Nature is a resource for the use of human beings. Natural resources are there for our use; the failure to use them is a form of waste.
- You can spend your money better than the government can.
- Freedom requires property rights: the rights to acquire, maintain, use, and dispose of property as you see fit.
- Cost-benefit analysis, as used by private industry, should govern public policy.
- Everybody with sufficient discipline can succeed. Anyone who is poor just hasn't had the discipline to use the free market to become prosperous and doesn't deserve any handouts.
- Economic freedom is the central freedom, since it leads

inevitably to other freedoms: free speech, free elections, civilian control of the military, civil liberties, checks and balances in government, a free press.

When conservatives speak of economic freedom and economic liberty, these are the kinds of ideas they have in mind—treating corporations as persons with individual, inalienable rights. In the economic mythology of the right, this metaphor is symbolized by the entrepreneur, the individual who starts a business, which might turn out to be a multibillion-dollar corporation. The entrepreneur stands for his corporation.

In this conception of freedom, there is a protagonist who is free. The protagonist—the hero of this story—is the entrepreneur, the individual who makes it. The market is like the magic sword of the fairy tales, the magical instrument working for good that enables the hero to succeed. The dragon to be slain and overcome—Grover Norquist's "beast"—is the government. The successful entrepreneur of the story has to overcome the government at every turn: minimize or avoid taxes; pay at least a minimum wage; accommodate to, or get around, environmental, safety, and fairness regulations; negotiate with unions according to labor laws; provide health benefits and pensions for workers; defend against consumer lawsuits when his products harm customers or the public.

Our hero gives people jobs and contributes to our standard of living, but he has to fight every inch of the way to do it. It is the economic freedom of the free market, along with his discipline, that allows him to succeed and get his reward, often a substantial one. But think of how much freer he could be, how much more good he could do, and how much more profit he could make (providing him even more freedom), if he didn't have to fight against the beast—the government that stands in his way limiting his freedom.

THE OWNERSHIP SOCIETY MYTH

In strict father morality, it is wrong to give people things they have not earned, because it makes them dependent and takes away their discipline, which is necessary for them to be moral and to become prosperous via the free market. Government social programs are therefore immoral, since they give people things they don't have, make them dependent on the government, and rob them of their discipline. The ownership society is a radical conservative utopia where all government social programs and safety nets have been eliminated and everyone has become free of dependence on government. In the place of Social Security and Medicare, there are private accounts that individuals invest with Wall Street brokers—at their own risk, since the stock market is very much a gamble.

In this utopia, every American—whether old or infirm or disabled or mentally ill—now has the incentive to develop discipline and does! All Americans develop discipline and become entrepreneurs and crafty investors. They all set up private stock portfolios that flourish because they have all become expert money managers. All Americans become homeowners, sign up for their own adequate health and retirement insurance, and own stocks, and many even own their own businesses. Everyone who wants to start a business can. The government shrinks and virtually disappears. It gets out of your way and stops spending your money. Its legitimate functions are privatized. The country prospers. This is the ownership society.

It is a myth.

THE TRUTHS HIDDEN BY
THE ECONOMIC LIBERTY MYTH

CORPORATIONS ARE GOVERNMENTS, NOT PERSONS

Large corporations act like governments—not persons—in many ways: They are highly bureaucratic and impersonal, can be extremely wasteful, and—via tax deductions for business expenses, tax breaks, and subsidies—use vast amounts of taxpayers' money, often in extravagant and wasteful ways. Because of patent law or the ability to buy out or drive out competitors, large corporations often consolidate their sovereignty over an industry and then, with competition highly restricted, can set high prices justified not by costs but by a desire for high profits. This is operation outside of the market, like a private government. When this happens, corporations have, essentially, the power to tax citizens, with money going to corporate profits—a form of taxation without representation.

Moreover, large corporations determine a great deal about the everyday lives of citizens—the possibilities for health care, the kind of news made available, the types of available communication systems, the kind of energy used, the type of transportation available, what food is available to eat and how safe it is. A big difference is that corporations are not accountable via elections or openness of operations to the general public.

In all these ways, large corporations do not act like persons, and the economic liberty myth should not be applying to them. But it does.

COMMONWEALTHS

As we have already seen, America's founders had a crucial idea: to pool the common wealth for the common good to build an infrastructure so that everyone could have the resources to achieve his or her individual goals. A government's job was to administer the common wealth to benefit all: to provide for a common defense, to be sure, but also to provide for roads, education, public buildings, and other forms of infrastructure that each citizen could use.

Today taxes provide the common wealth for a common infrastructure to serve individual needs and individual goals: freeways, paid for by taxpayer money; levees, holding back floodwater; the Internet, developed and administered with taxpayer money; public education at all levels; public libraries; the banking system, made dependable through taxpayer money; the court system, guaranteeing contracts; the SEC, governing the stock market. No one can start or run a business without the use of the common wealth—taxpayer money. Nobody makes it on his or her own in America. Everyone who succeeds uses some form of the common wealth used for the common good. There are no self-made men or women in America! The part of the economic liberty myth about individual initiative, individual responsibility, and pulling yourself up by your bootstraps is nonsense. Everyone uses the common wealth: That's what taxes are about—providing and maintaining the common infrastructure needed to realize our individual dreams.

THE CHEAP LABOR TRAP

Notice who is *not* the hero of the economic liberty myth: the forty-five million people who work for a living but can't even afford health care; indigent people who are too old or sick to work; the millions of middle-class workers whose wages have not gone up for thirty years while costs have risen steadily and their productivity has risen accordingly, with profits going to their companies, not to them. But there is a myth that links these Americans to the conservative hero story: Everyone can pull himself or herself up by the bootstraps! You too, the myth says, can be that hero. And if you're not, you have only yourself to blame.

As Sean Hannity said, "That's the thing about freedom. It doesn't guarantee success . . . But let's say you show a little self-discipline . . . you work really hard . . . you get out and hustle . . . I guarantee you. You'll be on the road to success."

The myth, of course, is false. As I have pointed out, forty-five million people cannot, all at once, pull themselves up by their bootstraps and become successful entrepreneurs or get better jobs. Those jobs are not there; the capital for starting that many businesses is not there. And anyway, who would do the necessary jobs that those forty-five million are performing now at low wages—picking fruit and vegetables, working in slaughterhouses, flipping burgers, waiting on tables, cleaning houses, caring for kids, doing day labor, cleaning buildings, pulling up weeds, washing cars—in short, doing the hundreds of jobs that pay very little but are absolutely necessary to our current lifestyles? A quarter of our working population is not even mentioned in the economic liberty myth. They hold up the lifestyles of the top three-quarters of our population, but they are caught in a cheap labor trap.

The trap is created via systemic causation by the structure of our economic system. Many factors come together to create it:

- The metaphor of labor as a resource whose costs are to be minimized
- Technology that allows the elimination of skilled jobs and the replacement of skilled by nonskilled workers
- The division of employees into assets that are valuable to the company and resources that are interchangeable and fungible
- The emphasis on short-term profits
- The outsourcing of resources to minimize their cost
- The offloading of labor onto customers—having customers put together furniture they buy, or bus their own

tables, or wade through tedious dial-up menus instead
of talking to a human service representative
- The flow of immigrants willing to do hard jobs for little
pay
- The consolidation of companies, which allows for lay-
ing off "redundant" workers
- The redistribution of wealth to the already wealthy

These and other factors create and maintain the trap in a complex way. If one thinks only in terms of direct causation, the trap
is invisible!

The cheap labor trap is the first of the progressive ideas
needed to tell the truth about economic freedom and the lack of
it in contemporary America. Even liberals who speak of the "two
Americas" do not want to confront an economic reality. Even if
the minimum wage were raised, the cheap labor trap would still
exist. The cheap labor trap is built into our economy. The economy is structured around low-wage jobs, and it tends to produce
more low-skill, low-wage jobs than high-skill, high-wage jobs.
Economic pressures for greater short-term profits for investors
have led to reorganizing the economy to reduce the skill level
needed for jobs, and with it, the level of wages. And as the skill
level is driven down, more of those jobs become exportable.

Given the lack of forty-five million higher-paying jobs at
their skill level, those working people will continue to be
trapped. Discipline is not bringing them opportunity. They have
little or no economic freedom and would have no more even if
the conservative agenda were fully realized.

LABOR AS A RESOURCE

Though these working Americans are not the heroes of the economic liberty myth, they are hidden in the story—as extras! Free

market economies have a "labor market," structured by the metaphor that labor is a resource to be bought and sold. Indeed, in the days of slavery, slaves were actually bought and sold. Today, large corporations have departments of "human resources" to hire, fire, and lay off workers who are seen as fungible, largely interchangeable—commodities, like coal and other raw materials.

Large corporations mostly have two classes of employees: the assets and the resources. The assets are the highly skilled, creative people—managers, economists, scientists, technology experts. These are hired by head-hunting agencies and get high salaries, stock options, and good benefits. The resources are low-skilled and hired routinely. Efficiency requires using fewer resources per unit of production to produce higher profits. Resource use is to be minimized, and that includes labor. This is part of the economic pressure maintaining a cheap labor trap. For labor resources to be cheaply available, there must be sufficient unemployment to keep the price of labor low in the labor market.

What is hidden in the economic liberty myth is that the myth both entails and *requires* a cheap labor trap. The market is a form of competition. In competitions, there will always be winners and losers. The hero in the economic liberty myth is a winner. What is hidden are the losers required by the myth and the unemployment required by the need for cheap labor.

UNIONS

The labor as resource metaphor is virtually omnipresent in business. An individual looking for a job with a large company is at a considerable disadvantage in negotiating terms. The company has all the power on its side to hold down wages and benefits. That is why the economic liberty myth sees unions as a threat to corporate profit and as a threat to corporate freedom in the market.

Unions attempt to level the playing field. They assume the metaphor that labor is a resource. Their objective is to corner the market on labor and drive up the price to the point where workers can get a fair shake in negotiations with management.

But what is crucial about unions is not the way they bargain for wages and benefits for their members, but what they contribute to society as a whole.

It is unions that have gotten us the five-day week and the eight-hour day, as well as safety regulations. In doing so, unions have contributed massively to our freedom.

MARKETS ARE CONSTRUCTED, NOT NATURAL

The economic liberty myth takes free markets as a natural phenomenon. But markets are constructed—usually for the benefit of those constructing and maintaining them. The World Trade Organization, for example, is hardly natural. It has hundreds of pages of rules governing its operation. Free markets are supposed to maximize the profit of everyone who partakes of them. When they don't do this, there is "market failure."

Markets are anything but natural, and they fail regularly for those whose interests they were not constructed to serve. The moral is that they should be constructed to serve the common good.

THE PROGRESSIVE WORK ETHIC

It is hardly news that Americans have a work ethic. It is a traditional progressive work ethic. Here are the often-hidden principles behind that work ethic.

- If you work for a living, you should earn a living.
- Work is a contribution to society in general.
- Work deserves to be compensated according to its contribution to society.
- Workers provide profits to business owners.
- A healthy society should have useful, fairly compensated work for everyone.

Americans on the whole believe that whoever does useful work should be able to earn a living at it, that they should be able to afford adequate food, clothing, housing, health care, and education for themselves and their children at a reasonable American standard of living. In short, there should be no cheap labor trap. It's simply un-American. In the world's richest nation, people should get paid adequately for their work. To put it in slogan form: If you work for a living, you should earn a living.

Try to imagine what life would be like if all the people who could not afford health care suddenly went on strike. The lifestyles of the top three-quarters of the population could not be maintained. The American standard of living depends on the people in the cheap labor trap. This thought experiment gives us a good idea of just how very much those caught in the cheap labor trap contribute to American society as a whole—not just to the people who pay their wages.

Fairness is a central value to Americans, and part of that is fair compensation for work done. Correspondingly, there is outrage when compensation is seen as too high—like CEO pay hundreds of times the salary of an ordinary worker. There is a sense that what you make should be in proportion to your contribution to society. Correspondingly, nobody complains when a Nobel Prize–winning biologist gets a million-dollar award. If his work is world class and makes a major contribution, then he should be paid well. Similarly, those in the cheap labor trap whose labor is essential to society as a whole should be making a decent living. The labor market is failing the fairness test.

WORKERS PROVIDE PROFITS

Part of the economic liberty myth is that employers "give jobs" to employees. The flip side of that is a deep truth: Working people provide profits to those who pay their wages, and it is the work by workers, even low-skilled workers, that provides profits to employers. In America over the past thirty years, wages have not risen much for the middle class, while efficiency and the corresponding profits and executive salaries have risen enormously. In short, the profits from productivity increases are not going to the workers who are being more productive. Instead they are going to owners and investors who are *not* doing the more productive work. That is unfair and un-American. Middle-class working people have been providing more and more profits to owners and investors without making higher and higher wages. An economy that works this way is immoral.

MORALITY AND MARKETS

Classical economics views markets as natural and amoral. They are not. All markets are constructed, and they are constructed in accord with certain values. The question is, Whose values? Markets that fit the economic liberty myth are constructed to fit strict father morality. But markets should be constructed for the common good, so that everybody will be able to reap their benefits. Markets are moral instruments. The question is, Whose morality are they structured to fit?

TRANSFERS OF WEALTH

Today, the top 2 percent of Americans own more assets than the bottom 80 percent. That is twice the assets they held thirty years ago. Yet the top 2 percent have by no means worked twice as much or twice as hard as the bottom 80 percent. What has happened over that period is that there has been a huge transfer of wealth to the wealthiest Americans, without it being earned through work. This is an overwhelming violation of the principles of a moral economy. And it is a violation of the economic liberty myth.

Moreover, conservative economic policies regularly sanction transfers of wealth from ordinary taxpayers to the wealthy, again outside of compensation for work. These transfers come in various forms:

- Corporate subsidies ($160 billion in December 2004) are transfers of wealth from ordinary taxpayers to investors in those corporations.
- What are called "tax cuts" that favor the wealthy— demanded by the Bush administration—are actually transfers of wealth from ordinary taxpayers to the wealthy.
- No-bid contracts to corporations like Halliburton and Bechtel are transfers of wealth from ordinary taxpayers to investors in those corporations. Since bids introduce competition and hence lower the cost to the public, no-bid contracts cost more and the difference is just a transfer of wealth to corporate investors.
- Below-market rate contracts for water, grazing, and mining rights on public lands are transfers of wealth from ordinary taxpayers to wealthy investors.

Such transfers of wealth to the wealthy are sanctioned by the economic liberty myth, by the ideas that privatization is always good and that nature is a resource for private use. In a moral economy, governed by the American work ethic, these are all impediments to freedom.

Recall that wealth confers freedoms. Transfers of wealth are transfers of freedom. When wealth is transferred from large numbers of ordinary taxpayers to a relatively small number of the extremely wealthy, freedom is being transferred as well from the many to the few.

TRANSFERS OF GOVERNING POWER

As we saw above, so-called private corporations, when they are large and powerful, act as governments over the general public. Their powers can extend to life and death, say, in the safety requirements of car manufacturers, drug companies, and food suppliers. HMOs govern what health care we can receive. Paper mills, agribusiness, and coal mining companies determine whether our drinking water is polluted. Communications companies decide what news we get and what entertainment is available. Most aspects of our lives are governed by the decisions made by large corporations. They are governments without accountability. We cannot elect new executives of such companies who will, on their own, improve our air and water quality; our automobile, drug, and food safety; and the range of news and opinion available to us.

We have traditionally relied on government regulation in such matters. But conservatives have gutted regulatory agencies, both by explicit deregulation or by de facto deregulation: taking away funding or shifting personnel away from regulation, as in the Environmental Protection Agency, the Food and Drug Administration, and the Justice Department. Deregulation does not produce less government. Deregulation simply transfers governing power from public forms of government, which are accountable to the public, to private forms of government, which lack accountability.

Corporations have the power to harm us, and harm interferes with our freedom. Government regulation, by being accountable to the public, restricts that power and allows the public greater freedom.

None of these truths about freedom are in the economic liberty myth. The reason is clear. The economic liberty myth presupposes the metaphor that corporations are persons. This allows not only the investors and managers of the corporation but also the corporation itself to fit the protagonist role in the myth. It is the corporation itself whose freedom from government control is at stake. It is the corporation that stands to gain full freedom—governing power without accountability—when deregulation and tort reform occur. But members of the public, who stand to lose freedom to the corporation, are outside the myth.

PROPERTY RESPONSIBILITIES

Property rights are at the center of the economic liberty myth. But for every right, there is a corresponding responsibility. And although conservatives tout personal responsibility, they say almost nothing about the property responsibilities that go with property rights. Yet property responsibilities have just as much to say about freedom as do property rights, but they are about the freedom of those affected by one's ownership of property.

There are obvious responsibilities that go with owning property. Take real estate. Owners have the responsibility to pay property taxes (to maintain roads, sewers, schools), to keep the property up to code (for public safety), and to carry insurance (to cover liability to others as well as oneself). Business owners have responsibilities to their customers (to treat them fairly, to make sure products are safe) and to their community (to do no harm, to perform community service, to contribute like other community members). And of course they have fiduciary responsibilities to their investors (honesty, openness, producing profits). And there are further responsibilities. If there is a stream on your property, you have a responsibility to your neighbors downstream not to pollute the stream, just as you have a responsibility to your neighbors not to pollute their air.

In short, property owners have a responsibility not to infringe on the freedom of their neighbors or the public.

THE CIVIL JUSTICE SYSTEM

In the economic liberty myth, freedom from lawsuits is a form of freedom from government interference in the market. At issue here is the civil justice system. Corporations have the power to do great harm, both to individuals and to the public at large. And as government deregulation proceeds, more and more governing power without accountability is placed in corporate hands, which gives corporations greater power to harm the public. Corporations are not subject to criminal prosecution; they cannot be put in jail or given the death penalty. But they can be sued. Only occasionally are corporate executives criminally liable and actually convicted.

When corporations harm members of the public, the civil justice system takes over where the criminal justice system leaves off. The civil justice system is best understood as a metaphorical version of the criminal justice system. In the civil justice system, the criminals are corporations, the victims are plaintiffs, the trial is a lawsuit, and there are a judge and a jury and a defense attorney. The biggest difference is that the roles of police, detectives, and prosecutor are all performed by trial lawyers, and the funding for the detective work and the prosecution all comes from attorneys' fees.

"Tort reform" would cap compensatory damages and either cap or eliminate punitive damages. The result would be to destroy the civil justice system altogether by making it financially impossible for trial lawyers to function as detectives and prosecutors. Given deregulation, the civil justice system is the last form of protection for the public against harmful corporate practices.

Since harm limits one's freedom, so-called tort reform is an attack on freedom for all Americans.

CULTURAL AND SOCIAL CAPITAL

The great French sociologist Pierre Bourdieu studied what he called "cultural capital" and "social capital." Cultural capital refers to the advantages in French society that come from the correct cultural background—upper-class family upbringing, having gone to the right schools, having worked in the right positions, and knowing the right people. Cultural capital also consists in things you know and know to do: how to speak well, what to wear, how to hold your fork, how to walk, what to do and not do to get ahead both economically and socially. Social capital constitutes the network of social relations that you enter into. Bourdieu pointed out that cultural and social capital play an enormous role in getting access to money and power.

The economic liberty myth says nothing of the role of cultural capital in financial success. It is about discipline, about pulling yourself up by your bootstraps, not about using your family connections and your upper-class background. The reason is that the economic liberty myth is a populist myth, meant to apply to ordinary poor and middle-class people who have strict father morality—though the myth actually benefits conservative elites the most.

THE ECONOMIC LIBERTY AND OWNERSHIP
SOCIETY MYTHS ARE SHAMS

To put it bluntly, the economic liberty and ownership society myths are shams. They hide truths that completely undermine them. Yet they are powerful and popular. They are powerful because they draw upon strict father morality, which defines self-identity for a great many Americans. They are popular because they have been repeated over and over for nearly thirty years by the right-wing message machine until they have changed the brains of tens of millions of Americans. The mere fact that they are fallacious is not sufficient to overcome their status as defining common sense for all those people. And arguing against them merely reinforces them.

Instead it is necessary to tell these truths in the form of a coherent progressive story. Here is an outline of what that story might be like.

The Progressive Story of Economic Freedom

- Since the days of the Commonwealths of Virginia and Massachusetts, it has been part of the genius of America to put together the common wealth for the common good to provide an infrastructure that everyone needs and can use to achieve his or her individual goals. That's what taxes are about, and without them we would not have that infrastructure: highways, the Internet, public education, scientific research, the banking and court systems, the stock market, public buildings, levees to hold back floodwaters. Without such an infrastructure, America would break down, no business could flourish, and there would be little or no individual success. Without the commonwealth—government for our common good—there would be no America.

- America has always had a progressive work ethic based on fairness: If you work for a living, you should earn a living. Work is a contribution to society in general, and those who work should be compensated for their contributions to our overall well-being. The cheap labor trap is immoral and we must find a way to eliminate it.

- Adequate early childhood education provides an essential form of cultural capital and it should be available free to all children.
- The vast transfers of wealth from ordinary taxpayers to the wealthy have been unconscionable and must be stopped and, if possible, reversed.
- The business of America is business. Trust is central to American business practice, and trust comes from the exercise of property responsibilities.
- Large corporations should be understood as being like governments—using vast amounts of taxpayers' money, bureaucratic, impersonal, often wasteful, and making decisions governing the everyday lives and the safety of the general public.
- Institutions that govern our lives should be accountable to the public. Governing power should not be transferred from publicly accountable forms of government to private, unaccountable forms of government.
- The civil justice system is there to protect us, and we must protect it.
- The great engines of wealth creation in America are public education and the diversity of ideas that starts with cultural diversity and the creativity it fosters.
- Markets are constructed and they are inherently moral instruments that should serve the common good.

These are the minimal guidelines for economic freedom, progressive style.

10

RELIGION AND FREEDOM

Religion has taken center stage in American politics. But it isn't just any religion: Fundamentalist Christians have made political issues out of abortion, gay marriage, stem-cell research, school prayer, the Pledge of Allegiance, evolution (and science in general), the separation of church and state, the right to proselytize, and even . . . Christmas! And they have done all this in the name of "freedom" and "liberty."

The basic difference between progressive and fundamentalist Christians is in their central metaphor for God. If God is seen as a nurturant parent, you get a progressive Christianity. If God is understood as a strict father, you get a fundamentalist Christianity.

As we have seen in general in the case of strict and nurturant moral models, we all have both models, either actively or passively. And many people are biconceptual, having one model active in some aspects of their lives and the other active in other aspects of life. We expect nothing less of religion: views in which God is conceptualized as fully nurturant (the Unitarian Universalists), views in which God is conceptualized as fully strict (the fundamentalists of various denominations), and views where God is conceptualized as nurturant in some respects and strict in others.

Fundamentalists are a minority of American Christians, but

they wield enormous organizational, political, and media power. One of their most powerful weapons is language—language that makes it seem as if they are not just the typical Christians, but the real Christians, the ones who read the Bible literally and correctly and act from moral convictions to promote the Truth of the Gospel. They deploy a simple logic: Americans are mostly Christians, fundamentalists are both typical Christians and ideally moral Christians, therefore they are both typical and ideally moral Americans. They seem to want the word "Christian" to mean fundamentalist. And they are in the process of convincing the media of that logic: To be a good American is to be a good Christian is to be a fundamentalist Christian, whose idea of freedom is the correct view of freedom—the Gospel Truth. It is all empirically false, but if they can establish this frame, the truth won't matter.

To keep conservative Christians from dominating the religious discourse, we need to understand a set of complicated issues: What, exactly, are the differences between progressive and conservative Christianity? How does the concept of freedom differ in these traditions? And how do these differences show up in politics?

To understand these issues, even at a basic level, we will need a bit of background. The contemporary discourse about religion and politics uses ideas like virtue, character, and morality. We need to understand better what is meant by these ideas in the progressive and conservative Christian traditions. In addition, there are two ideas that are central to the fundamentalist tradition: essence and teleology.

ESSENCE

Human beings around the world tend to have a common folk theory of nature in which everything in the world is a *kind* of thing, a member of a category. We attribute to each kind of thing an essence, some property or set of properties that makes something the kind of thing it is. Essences are part of the nature of things; things would not be what they are without their essences. Elephants wouldn't be elephants without trunks, horses wouldn't be horses without hooves, chairs wouldn't be chairs without seats (or a surface to sit on).

Essences define the kinds of things there are in the world. It is assumed that everything has a given essence or it doesn't. That means that categories have clear boundaries. Every animal is either an elephant or it isn't.

Essences have causal powers: They determine the natural behavior of things. Part of the essence of a tree is to be made of wood, which is a substance that behaves in a certain way: It burns, you can carve it with a knife, etc. Therefore, a tree will burn and it can be carved with a knife.

In classical Greek philosophy, essences were typically divided into substance, form, and pattern of change. Trees are made of a substance: wood. Trees have a form: roots, trunk, limbs, branches, leaves, and fruit. Trees have a pattern of change: They grow from seeds, sprout, grow tall and develop a limb structure, grow leaves, and eventually die and fall over.

The natural behavior of trees is seen as following from these essences: They burn because they are made of wood, you can climb them because they have a trunk and limbs, and you can plant and cultivate them because they develop from seeds and bear fruit.

According to the theory of essences, the oak is already there in the acorn, since the pattern of change is inherent in the acorn: The acorn will naturally develop into the oak. Apply this to people: The person is there in the fertilized egg—at conception—since the fertilized egg, in the womb, will naturally develop into a child.

This idea, as we will see, is central to debates over abortion and stem-cell research.

TELEOLOGY

Teleology is the idea that things don't just happen; they are part of some larger coherent whole that has a built-in purpose or an end state that events are moving toward. Typically, you do not know what that purpose or end state is.

Teleology for living things is bound up with the notion of flourishing, doing well given the kind of thing you are. Thus, flowers are supposed to grow and bloom, fish are supposed to swim, birds (not counting penguins and ostriches) are supposed to fly and sing their songs—and all three are supposed to grow and reproduce.

Evolution explains this without teleology, of course: Things that flourish in their habitat tend to survive. But science or no science, people will always think in terms of teleology, because that is how the human mind works. Take a sentence such as "We developed thumbs so that we could pick things up better." This is teleological thinking. It assumes that it was determined in advance that human beings should be able to pick things up easily, and that thumbs developed so that this end state could be realized.

If you see a complex organism made up of simple parts that function in an ingenious way, like the human eye, you may well view it—using teleology—as having an "intelligent design" created by a "designer." This designer put together from scratch all the individual elements of the eye so that it could fulfill its purpose, which is to see. In the fundamentalist tradition, that designer is God.

Teleology as a folk theory is widespread around the world. It arises naturally, first because there really are in the world a great many natural processes with natural end states, and second because *we* have plans and purposes and we tend to project the notion of plans and purposes onto the world. In fundamentalist religion, teleology appears as God's plan, and all of creation is unfolding according to God's plan.

VIRTUE ETHICS

Aristotle made the ideas of essences, teleology, and flourishing central to his theory of ethics—virtue ethics. Flourishing for an individual person is that person fulfilling his or her potential—developing and using his or her gifts to best advantage and becoming happy through doing so. Aristotle, the founder of systematic biology, understood that just as plants need to be cultivated in order to flourish, so human beings need some "cultivation" as well. Aristotle believed that people could develop certain traits—called virtues—that would help them flourish and be happy. These are personal virtues, since they apply to individuals. What is flourishing for one person may not be flourishing for another, and so different people may require different personal virtues.

Other virtues are social in nature, as required for a good society, for example, honesty and compassion. A good society, for Aristotle, is one that helps people fulfill their potential and flourish. Here we see a precursor to progressive thought, to the idea that the state has a responsibility to help citizens flourish and that good citizenship—civic virtue—is required for the state to fulfill that function.

Notice that virtue ethics uses the ideas of essence and teleology for individuals, as well as for people in general. Different people have different essences and thus different natural modes of flourishing. And of course, there are vices as well as virtues. The potential to be a liar, a thief, or a murderer—that is, one who interferes with the flourishing of others—does not count as worthy of flourishing.

MORAL LAW

Virtue ethics contrasts sharply with moral law, an approach to morality in which certain actions are defined as absolutely right and others as absolutely wrong. There are many systems of moral laws, both in America and around the world. They all have lists of rules to follow.

Virtue ethics does not require such a list of rules. In moral law theory, obedience to the law, performing an action prescribed as "right," may very well conflict with flourishing and happiness, and with what virtue ethics considers a good society. If it does, then flourishing, happiness, and the good society are seen as wrong, and doing what will make you flourish or your society "good" can be considered evil.

Consider, for example, assisting with the suicide of a patient with a terminal disease, horrible pain, no hope of recovery, and nothing to live for. A particular system of moral law may ban assisted suicide, but in a system of virtue ethics, the virtues of empathy and responsibility may see it as moral in such a case. Or consider a fetus that develops with a genetic defect that leaves it with no brain. If born without a brain, it would soon die outside the womb and, even with life support, could never lead anything like a human life. Suppose, in addition, that the birth would endanger the life of the mother. Abortion is banned by some systems of moral law, but under virtue ethics, the virtues of empathy and responsibility may very well lead one to see terminating the pregnancy as highly moral in such a case.

Many people live by a moral law that requires absolute nonviolence, and yet in some situations violence may be required to save the lives of others. In such a case, under virtue ethics, empathy for a potential murder victim could declare certain violence moral, where the given moral law would not.

Moral law very often requires discipline and sacrifice, because what is best for your individual flourishing, and even survival, can violate some precept of moral law. This is a form of discipline—*negative* discipline—that can be diametrically opposed to your flourishing. Virtue ethics also requires discipline, but it is usually a different kind: one that supports and makes possible flourishing—*positive* discipline.

Within the idea of moral law, developing "character" is developing negative discipline—the moral strength to say no to your desires and to make sacrifices for the sake of obeying the moral law. Virtue, in a moral law system, consists in obeying moral laws, and virtues are traits that help you obey moral laws even under difficult conditions. This is what is meant by virtues when used by ultraconservative writers like William Bennett and Rick Santorum. They are social virtues appropriate for all, rather than personal virtues, which are not taken seriously by conservatives. As Dick Cheney said in rejecting the very idea of including conservation of energy as government policy, "Conservation may be a sign of personal virtue, but it is not a sufficient basis for a sound, comprehensive energy policy."

Character is very different in virtue ethics than in a morality based on moral law: Character consists in having the right social virtues—empathy, responsibility, honesty, etc.—as well as the focus and the energy, to function virtuously under trying circumstances and not give up.

Causation is also a part of character in the two models. Moral law is about direct causation, about individuals obeying the law, about individual action or individual ability to refrain from action. Character in moral law requires the ability to control direct causation. Character in virtue ethics is about both direct and systemic causation, the ability to understand the complexity of social systems, to judge complex situations, to understand the complex effects of one's actions, and then to do what is most ethical according to both personal and social virtues.

Virtue ethics and moral law are both moral systems. Neither is relativistic, neither says that anything goes. Virtue ethics has the advantage of promoting a recognition of systemic causation and hence of allowing many complex realities to be recognized that might be ignored under moral law. And there are systems where both occur and one is given priority.

Essence, teleology, virtue ethics, and moral law are everyday ideas that have shaped philosophy and, in so doing, have had a major impact on religion and politics.

We are now in a position to see how these ideas function in progressive and conservative Christianity—and in politics.

Let us begin our discussion with progressive Christianity. It is the Christianity of American freedom—of the abolitionists, the suffragists, and the civil rights movement.

PROGRESSIVE CHRISTIANITY

Progressive Christians see God as a nurturant parent, offering unconditional love and grace. Grace, for progressive Christians, is metaphorical nurturance: You have to be close to God to get grace, you can't earn grace, you have to actively accept grace to get it, you are filled with grace, you are healed by grace, you are made a moral being by grace. Christ, in the progressive tradition, offers a model for living—the embodiment of the progressive values of empathy and responsibility. Progressive Christians tend to focus not on the apocalyptic strain of the New Testament but on Jesus' acts and the values they represent.

These values are tied up with flourishing and with a kind of virtue ethics. If you empathize with someone, you want him or her to flourish. If you are responsible to yourself and others, you want to work for a society that maximizes flourishing for all. God's grace—His nurturance—helps you flourish. You can't earn grace, but you can do what is necessary: get close to God, by following in Christ's footsteps and living a Christian life.

What is a Christian life, one lived according to the moral teachings of Jesus? Renounce violence (turn the other cheek), don't try to dominate others (the meek shall inherit the earth), be tolerant (judge not lest ye be judged), offer forgiveness (who will cast the first stone?), love your neighbor as yourself, heal the sick, help the poor and helpless.

The idea, of course, is that everyone should live this way— and if they did, the result would be . . . freedom! Freedom from violence, domination, intolerance, vengeance, hatred, illness, poverty, and helplessness. If everyone turned the other cheek, we would all be free from violence. If no one tried to dominate others, we would all be free of domination. If no one was judgmental, we would be free of intolerance. And so on. Jesus preached progressive freedom, freedom from oppression, what today is called social justice.

But progressive Christianity is not just about freedom from. It is also about freedom to—being free to flourish. "Love thy neighbor as thyself." Show empathy and act on it, take responsibility: do what you can to help your neighbor flourish. And if everyone does that, your neighbors will help you flourish. Progressive Christianity is about members of a community—and citizens of a nation—maximizing the freedom for everyone to become his or her best self. "The meek shall inherit the earth." Why? If everyone were to stop trying to dominate others, if everyone became "meek," people would not impose on the freedom of others and so would maximize the freedom of everyone to prosper. It is the logic of Jesus and the logic of progressives.

Progressive Christianity is a religion of progressive freedom— American freedom. Its God is a nurturant God. Its morality is nurturant morality. It has the goal of creating a good society, one that helps people fulfill their potential and flourish. Its politics is progressive politics: The state's responsibility is to secure citizens' freedom through doing everything it can to assure the right care, build the right institutions, and create the right experiences— nurturant child rearing, progressive schools, good health care, caring communities, good jobs—while avoiding all the wrong ones—being raised in poverty, ignorance, violence, and joblessness.

Realizing the values of Jesus in the world requires not just personal action but also political action—action through the state. The politics of progressive religion is not narrowly about matters of the church; it is about the broadest range of issues that have an effect on human flourishing. Today, following in the footsteps of Jesus means being a political activist as well as a virtuous individual. Unfortunately, most progressive Christians do not understand the political implications of their theology.

CHURCH AND STATE

The morality of progressive Christianity says a great deal about the relationship between the state and religion. A state religion would impose force and control on religious values and practice, and impinge on matters of individual conscience. State recognition would introduce political control and political advantage, either advantaging one religion over another or making religion something other than purely a matter of conscience. Favoring religion over nonreligion again introduces matters of force, control, or advantage, where only matters of conscience—your relationship to God—should enter. From these considerations, it appears that progressive Christianity is committed to the following views.

- There should be no state religion and no state recognition of any version of any religion.
- The separation of church and state should be maintained; the government should not favor any religion over any other, nor favor religion over nonreligion.
- The government should not interfere in the practice of

any religion, except if that practice criminally harms people, interferes with the freedoms of others, or endangers public safety.

- The practice of religion should remain separate from public life.
- No religion should impose itself on anyone or engage in any coercive practice.
- No religion's views should be made part of the curriculum in any public school.
- No pressure from superiors or peers to join a religion or join in the practice of any religion should occur in any public institution.
- There should be no favoritism based on religion in employment, in promotions, or in evaluations in any institution receiving public funds or using public facilities.

Progressive Christians read the Bible to obtain moral lessons for everyday life, and they understand that it teaches via metaphor and parable. And what it teaches are the traditional values of progressive American freedom.

Life is a progressive issue, since progressive Christians are committed to promoting freedom, freedom from oppression and pain and freedom to realize one's dreams. Progressive Christians promote an inherent, though undeclared, "culture of life." They tend to favor minimizing infant mortality by having the state pay for pre- and postnatal care for indigent women; universal health care; care for the elderly; cleaning up, and stopping, pollution to advance health and life; ending the death penalty; and most important, diplomacy over war.

Progressive Christians recognize and respect the difficulty of the decision faced by women with unwanted pregnancies. They do not favor the government intruding on its citizens' freedom to make their own, and their families', medical decisions for them. Remember why freedom is visceral. Freedom is about the body and one's own control of it. For most women, abortion is a freedom issue, since it is about control over their own bodies.

There are two possible constitutional issues here. First, is the freedom to control your own body and make your own medical decisions protected by the Constitution? Second, should advocates of conservative Christianity be able to restrict such a freedom on the part of those of another religious persuasion?

Nobody wants unwanted pregnancies. Progressive Christians, like women everywhere, would like to minimize unwanted pregnancies—not by force but by addressing many of the reasons for unwanted pregnancies, that is, by having government fund sex education, contraception in schools, and family planning; increasing funding for adoption and foster care; and funding child-rearing expenses for the indigent. These pro-life policies are all opposed by the radical right and fundamentalist Christians.

Progressive Christians also tend to want to protect women who are raped and get pregnant as a result. At present, the number of such cases is roughly twenty-five thousand per year! This is an astonishingly large number and should make us pause to ask whether the state, by banning abortions or making them hard to obtain, should force tens of thousands of women a year to bear the children of their rapists—or have to try to find and finance unsafe and often deadly back-alley abortions. Progressive Christians tend not to want the state to force women into such horrible predicaments. The consequence of that is requiring that there be safe, cheap, and readily available facilities for terminating such pregnancies all over the country, as well as morning-after pills at rape crisis centers.

The point is simple: Progressive Christians care about life and health, and in the case of abortion tend to prefer prevention whenever possible and safe, inexpensive facilities whenever necessary.

Jimmy Carter, in *Our Endangered Values: America's Moral Crisis*, offers a clear and powerful description of progressive Chris-

tian values. A progressive evangelical Christian, Carter delivers
a spirited defense of progressive Christianity and an attack on
the dangers of fundamentalism and its political role. Carter ar-
gues forcefully that being a Christian has led him to the conclusion that government should work to keep a strong wall between
church and state, to respect science and religion as separate domains and to support science, to promote tolerance, to advance
the cause of women, to help the poor, to preserve the environment, to avoid preemptive war and abide by just war principles,
to avoid torture, to abolish the death penalty, to stop testing nuclear weapons, to ban the sale of assault weapons, to promote sex
education and family planning, and to support stem-cell research.

This is the Christianity of the America that people around
the world, of all religions, came to love and respect—until recently. It is the Christianity that stands for peace and hope and
prosperity for all. It is the Christianity that cares about people
everywhere, that respects human dignity, that deplores human
oppression. It is the Christianity that goes beyond mere tolerance to embrace people of goodwill of all religions, or of none.
As Carter explains, Christian values are currently under attack
in the name of Christianity.

Throughout American history, progressive Christians have
championed the expansion of American freedoms. America
needs progressive Christians to return to their great political heritage, to stem the fundamentalist tide, and to make freedom
mean freedom again.

FUNDAMENTALIST CHRISTIANITY

Fundamentalist Christians are politically conservative. Why?
Why couldn't they have their religious views but be politically

progressive, or independent? How do their religious views relate to their politics? How are they distinct from progressive Christians? What do fundamentalist Christians mean by "freedom" and "liberty," and how does that meaning fit with what these terms mean to right-wing political leaders?

There is a single answer to all these questions: strict father religion.

Judaism, Christianity, and Islam all have both strict and nurturant versions, which differ as to whether God is a strict father or a nurturant parent. In fundamentalist Christianity, God is a strict father. There is a strict good-evil divide in the world, where God is good and Satan is evil. God is the ultimate and absolute moral authority who issues commandments specifying what is right and wrong, and morality is obedience to these commandments. Going to heaven is the reward for obedience; going to hell is the punishment for disobedience.

The Bible, the word of God, is literally true and provides instruction for how to live. Everyone is born a sinner and would go to hell, except for Jesus' offer of redemption. Those who take him as savior are redeemed—Jesus pays off the moral debt for their sins and they are as if they were "born again." Now, if they obey, they go to heaven and achieve eternal happiness in God's presence; otherwise, they go to hell and undergo eternal suffering in alienation from God. In short, this is a religion based around the idea of individual responsibility, where each person is responsible for his or her own ultimate salvation. Obedience to the word of God takes discipline, and those without that discipline will perish in hell, and deserve to. Remember that "character" in this view is the capacity to be obedient to the moral law, to measure the effects of one's actions against what is prescribed by the strict father.

STRICTNESS AND ESSENCE

Strict father morality assumes that there is a clear division between right and wrong actions, and that there are rules (or laws or commandments) that determine which actions are right and which are wrong. Such rules mention kinds of agents and objects. The categories of agents and objects must have clear divisions as well, so that the commandments will either apply to them or not. If you have a rule that says women must wear dresses, you have to have criteria for what is a woman and what is a dress. Those criteria are essences—properties that make something the kind of thing it is. Strict father morality requires some version of the folk theory of essences.

Since fundamentalism takes God as a strict father, it too must assume a folk theory of essences. The right actions fit God's commandments; the wrong ones violate them. It is God who determines what is good. God is therefore the essence of goodness itself, and what He does must be good. Since God is all-powerful, His purpose in the world is God's plan. The world is thus given a teleology.

Here is some of the reasoning that comes out of the folk theories of essence and teleology when God is brought into this picture.

Women can have children and men cannot. It is therefore part of the essence of women to have children. Since God made men and women, it must have been part of God's plan for women to have children. Therefore, a woman who chooses to have an abortion is acting against her essence and in violation of God's plan.

Moreover, in fundamentalist Christianity, the soul—not the body—is the essence of a person. Thus, a person whose body dies can live on through eternity, because the soul can be separated from the body. Thus, the soul is not material. Absolute categories of right and wrong behavior make possible a clear distinction between heaven and hell.

These ideas, taken as absolute truth, explain part of the fervor over abortion and stem-cell research. Suppose you believe in the soul, and you believe that the soul is within, and animates, that is, gives life to, the person. Since a fetus is animated in the woman's womb, by this reasoning, it must have a soul. Since categories defined by essences are absolute and don't change, it follows, if you believe in essences, that the baby as born must have been a baby with a soul—not a mere fetus—all the way back to conception. The same must apply to a blastocyst, the hollow sphere containing only stem cells that stem-cell research is performed on. It too must be a baby—even though it has only stem cells and no bone cells, skin cells, nerve cells, organ cells, brain cells, or any other kind of cell. If God creates each person and places a unique soul within each fertilized egg at conception— for His purpose, which we cannot know—then abortion and stem-cell research are not only baby killing, but they also thwart God's plan in creating each of those souls. People who are trying to end abortion and stem-cell research therefore see themselves as serving God's plan.

Serving God's plan is not a light matter if you believe that only those who serve God's plan get to go to heaven and experience eternal bliss; all others go to hell and experience eternal pain and torture.

We can now see what the fuss over evolution is about. It is not just about some scientific subject matter or other for schools that happens to contradict fundamentalist religion. It is rather about who we are, given that we are largely defined by our deepest assumptions about the world: what we understand God to be (if there is one), what is God's plan for you (if He has one), and whether you will go to heaven or hell (if they exist) for all eternity.

Evolution says that we evolved through stages from lower animals, and that the process was not governed by any purpose at all. It denies that who we are as human beings had anything to do with God's plan. It denies teleology—that God even had a plan.

Because evolution says that species can develop into other species, it denies essence, which is unchanging. Evolution also denies absolute categorization, which is necessary not only for fundamentalist religion but also for strict father morality, which determines cultural values. If you identify yourself essentially as a fundamentalist Christian, then evolution denies your very identity!

ESSENCE, TELEOLOGY, AND FREEDOM

What does all this have to do with Freedom? Everything.

In fundamentalist religion, heaven is the ultimate freedom—from pain, suffering, and privation. "Free at last, free at last! Thank God Almighty, I'm free at last." You get there by acting according to your essence and in accord with God's plan.

Pope Benedict XVI has written extensively about religion and freedom from the perspective of Catholic fundamentalism. Essence and teleology, he notes, have causal force. When you act against what you most essentially are, when you act against what you were meant to do, it is like swimming upstream or walking uphill. You are going against the natural force of existence, you are taking on a burden that restricts your freedom. So a woman who has an abortion is acting against her essence and has given up her freedom. She has also taken away the fetus's freedom to live. So, the pope would argue, she has acted against freedom in two ways.

In addition, he links freedom and truth. Since God's word is truth, when you act against God's word you are acting against truth and the force of reality—again imposing upon yourself the burden of running up against reality, which limits your freedom.

Benedict XVI, like many fundamentalists, likes to rail against the classical Enlightenment view of freedom as the autonomy that comes from reason. Reason, in the Enlightenment view, is our essence, what makes us human beings. Because we all have reason, which is universal, we do not need to follow the dictates of external authorities like the king or the church. Morality, it is argued, follows from universal reason. In this view, reason alone gives us morality and hence makes us moral and autonomous—not in need of religion.

Benedict XVI, like most Protestant fundamentalists, assumes that morality and moral norms can come only from religion. Freedom cannot come from reason alone but requires religious morality. Here are some typical quotations:

> An understanding of freedom which tends to regard liberation exclusively as the ever more sweeping annulment of norms and the constant extension of individual liberties to the point of complete emancipation from all order is false. Freedom, if it is not to lead to deceit and self-destruction, must orient itself by the truth, that is, by what we really are, and must correspond to our being . . . Right is therefore not antithetical to freedom, but is a condition, indeed, a constitutive element of freedom itself . . .
>
> We must also lay to rest once and for all the dream of the absolute autonomy and self-sufficiency of reason. Human reason needs the support of the great religious traditions of humanity . . . Where God is denied, freedom is not built up, but robbed of its foundation and thus distorted . . . Where the purest and deepest religious traditions are entirely discarded, man severs himself from his truth, he lives contrary to it and becomes unfree . . . Even philosophical ethics cannot be unqualifiedly autonomous. It cannot renounce the idea of God or the idea of a truth of being having an ethical character. If there is no truth about man, man also has no freedom. Only the truth makes us free.

Truth here is God's truth, the truth set forth by religion. Freedom here is strict father freedom, requiring obedience to a moral authority—God. Since the church is the true interpreter of God's word, one of Benedict XVI's basic claims follows: You are most free when you are following the dogma of the church.

The Protestant fundamentalist version of this is that God made you (gave you an essence) and has a plan for you. You discover that plan by reading the Bible, going to church, and following the interpretations provided by your minister. If you go against your essence and God's plan, you will not only have difficulties on earth, but you will not get into heaven and will suffer eternal torture. You will be most free if you act according to your essence and follow God's plan for you.

Evangelical fundamentalist Christians believe it is their mission to convert people to their version of religion—to spread the "good news" about Jesus' offer of redemption. They believe that only they are the true "Christians," that Christians are better than non-Christians, that only Christians are going to heaven, that human law should be consistent with God's law, that the word of God is true and right, that the teachings of their church represent God's law, that social norms should fit God's law, and that, in a Christian nation, the power of the state should uphold God's law! They tend, therefore, to be social conservatives, who apply strict father morality to social life.

FUNDAMENTALISM AND CONSERVATISM

We are now in a position to answer the question asked above: What does fundamentalist Christianity have to do with right-wing politics? Adherents to both use strict father morality:

- Both have a clear division between right and wrong, good and evil. In fundamentalist Christianity, wrong is personified by the devil and evil spirits, and in hundreds of churches rituals to exorcise the devil take place. Conservatives have political devils—Communists, Islamic terrorists, and liberals, who are the worst of all since they undermine strict father morality itself. Both have the view that, in the words of George W. Bush, "If you're not with us, you're against us."

- Both see morality as obedience to a moral authority, ultimately God, but on earth a minister or the president—if he has the right moral views.
- Both see discipline as central to morality and the market as the way for disciplined, moral people to be rewarded. Both believe that undisciplined, immoral people do not deserve to be rewarded but should be punished—with poverty (conservatives) and with everlasting hell (fundamentalist Christians).
- Both see individual responsibility—not social responsibility—as central. For fundamentalists, each individual is to be judged by God on the basis of his own acts; everyone has individual responsibility. For economic conservatives, everyone has individual economic responsibility.
- Both have a notion of redemption. For economic conservatives, it lies in the market; there is always an opportunity to get rich. For fundamentalists, it lies in being born again, taking Christ as your savior, having your sins washed away and getting a new chance at everlasting life.
- In both, the defense and promulgation of the strict father worldview itself are the highest moral priorities. The worldview must be defended against all criticism, and it must be spread as widely as possible—both at home and abroad. Both are on evangelical missions to spread the "good news" and the truth of their strict father worldview.

- This highest priority, to defend and promulgate the strict father worldview, creates culture wars both at home and abroad. The danger in the United States to strict father morality is nurturant morality. Since strict and nurturant values are mutually inconsistent on most issues, the flourishing of progressive values is viewed as an attack on both conservative and fundamentalist values. Progressivism is thus seen as an enemy to be wiped out—both politically and religiously.

- Both identify with a literal, "originalist" reading of the founding documents—the Constitution and the Bible—as indicating the intentions of the Founding Fathers and God the Father, creators, respectively, of the nation and the world and the moral authorities we should follow today by reading their words with their original meaning.

- Since both see morality as obedience to a moral authority, with an absolute right and wrong, they mistake nurturant morality—based on empathy and responsibility for oneself and others—as having no morality at all. Both therefore attack progressives as "relativists" who place no constraints on moral behavior.

- Both believe that freedom is not absolute but presupposes a social order. That order arises from the internal discipline individuals need to obey commandments or laws. That discipline, after one is born again, permits one to remain spiritually free: free of sin and hence free to go to heaven and free from the torments of hell. In the market, that discipline allows one to gain the freedoms that money and property can bring.

- Correspondingly, both believe that government social programs take away the individual discipline needed to be both moral and prosperous.

- Both believe that morality derives from religion.

- Fundamentalists believe that their religion is the only true religion, that the Bible is literally true, and their reading of the Bible is literal truth. It follows that proselytizing is truth-telling, educating others as to the true nature of things, and that fundamentalist religion is therefore an essential part of education—the most important part of education. Conservatives similarly believe that of political and economic conservatism.
- "Freedom *of* religion" therefore could not possibly mean "freedom *from* religion." It can mean only the "freedom of religion to proselytize"—to tell its truths aloud in all public places and to try as hard as possible to bring others to recognize that truth.
- Since both fundamentalist religion and conservative politics are based on strict father morality, both understand that "traditional family values" (that is, strict father values) form the basis of conservative politics and fundamentalist Christianity. That's what holds them together.

Because both political progressives and progressive Christians have not understood the role of nurturant morality in their religion and their politics, the entire field of religion and politics has been left almost exclusively to conservatives. They have taken good advantage of the lack of strong opposing voices. And they have created a set of symbolic issues linking strict father morality to both religion and politics.

Abortion is not a "life" issue for right-wing Christians, though it may be for others. So-called pro-life conservatives are typically in favor of the death penalty. As we have seen, they favor conservative policies that result in America having the highest infant mortality rate in the industrialized world—twelve per one thousand births, which is almost three times the average of 4.5 per thousand. These deaths are a result of conservative policies against prenatal and postnatal care, universal child health insurance, Medicaid, programs guaranteeing adequate food and shelter for poor children. They favor energy policies that result in high pollution rates and an asthma epidemic in our cities, and in mercury poisoning in our streams and ocean waters so high that fish caught in streams cannot be eaten in forty-eight of the fifty states and that one out of six women of childbearing age have so much mercury in their bodies that they would be ill-advised to bear children, and when they do, there is high incidence of neurological disorders.

If they were really pro-life above everything, they would support programs for pre- and postnatal care, universal health care for all children, programs to feed and house hungry and homeless children, antipollution programs, and safe food programs. Instead, they let strict father morality dominate over issues of life—that the poor are responsible for their own poverty and that they and their innocent children should suffer for it, and that government should not interfere with corporate profits through public health regulations for clean air and water.

If life in general is not the paramount issue, what is really going on in the case of abortion? The same thing that is going on in gay marriage.

Abortion and gay marriage are symbolic issues for fundamentalists. That is why they are paired, even though they literally have nothing to do with each other. Both of them, symbolically, represent threats to the very idea of a strict father family—and threats to their idea of freedom.

The strict father model of the family is strongly gendered. The parents cannot be gay—one must be male and the other must be female. Only daddy and not mommy can protect and support the family, be strict enough to discipline the children, and be strong enough to be a moral authority. If your very identity is based on your role in a strict father family, then your identity will certainly be threatened by gay marriage.

The abortion issue functions symbolically in a similar way. The issue is about who has the moral authority over family life. In a strict father family, the father is the moral authority and makes the ultimate decisions on all important matters. If the daughter seeks an abortion, then she has acted immorally and should be punished by having to bear the consequences of her actions, even bearing the child if her father decides, or getting beaten or thrown out of the house in extreme, but all too prevalent, cases.

To say that women should make such decisions themselves is an affront to strict father morality. Again, suppose your very identity, as either a man or a woman, is defined by strict father morality. The very idea that a woman can make such a decision—a decision over her own reproduction, over her own body, and over a man's progeny—contradicts and represents a threat to the idea of strict father morality.

The right has defined abortion and gay rights as "the moral issues"—rather than, say, poverty, the destruction of the environment, the deficit that burdens future generations, nuclear proliferation, starting a war on false premises, torture, spying on fellow citizens, or honesty and openness in government, which are among the major moral issues that confront our society. They have been made "moral issues" because their symbolic values have powerful political effects that favor the radical right. They have become "the moral issues" only because progressives have allowed right-wing conservatives to monopolize talk of morality and virtue. Progressives can no longer afford to do that.

These issues are now being cast as a battle over the heart of American life—freedom. Freedom of religion and freedom of speech come together as freedom to proselytize. The separation of church and state becomes freedom from religion—the opposite of freedom of religion, enshrined in our Constitution. Upholding the separation of church and state is seen, therefore, as an "attack on religion"—a freedom guaranteed by the Constitution. When Democrats criticize a court pick for bringing religion into the public sphere, they are attacked as "anti-Christian" and "antireligion."

The removal of overt Christian symbols from public places—including "Merry Christmas" signs in store windows—is seen as such an attack. Jerry Falwell, taking the word symbolically for the thing, has framed this as an attack on Christmas itself, as if America's most beloved holiday—a holiday celebrated by most Americans—were itself under attack, instead of the use of religious words and symbols in prominent public places.

Freedom of speech becomes the freedom to teach the truth of the Gospel, including intelligent design in science classes, and freedom of access to information becomes the freedom of students to have access to opposing views, as if intelligent design and evolution were just opposing theories. Intelligent design is a current battleground for fundamentalists. But evolution is not the central issue. As intelligent design advocates at the Discovery Institute, their main center of institutional support, point out, the deeper attack is on real science as real scientists carry it out. Science, which looks to nature for natural causes and natural explanations, is referred to as "materialism."

Fundamentalists supporting intelligent design take the idea of materialism to be the real enemy. They see it as amoral, relativist, and antireligious, underlying the scientific approach to understanding reality. Since materialism accepts only material and not spiritual explanations for physical phenomena, it makes the implicit claim that God cannot be taken as an explanation for any events in the world or as an explanation for anything physical that exists—such as the physical world itself and all the living things in it.

It is not an accident that materialism involves systemic causation; thermodynamics and quantum mechanics require systemic causation, as does evolutionary biology. On the other hand, the idea that God intervenes in the physical world is an instance of direct causation. The issue of causation is central to science, and it is not surprising to find the strict father/nurturant parent dichotomy determining the kinds of causation accepted by fundamentalists.

Science *does* challenge, not religion in general but fundamentalist religion, which insists that its reading of the Bible is not a reading but an absolute truth about the nature of reality. Most religious people in America do not require such a fundamentalist understanding of the Bible; they read the Bible instead as providing important and useful stories and parables for understanding and guiding one's life—metaphorical stories that represent a moral but not necessarily a literal truth, stories that offer spiritual and moral insight but not a true account of all reality.

For both fundamentalists and scientists, an attack on truth is an attack on freedom. Since fundamentalist religion says that it has the absolute truth of the Gospel, and since their practice of religion requires that that truth be spread as far and as wide as possible, it should follow that freedom of religion, freedom of speech, and freedom of access to the truth should require intelligent design—its truth—to be taught in public school science classes as an alternative to evolution, the most highly established science we have.

Freedom of inquiry says otherwise, that evolution is the one and only overwhelmingly established, true account of how life was formed and how species got here. Progressive morality, and the politics it is based on, insists on responsibility—and it is irresponsible, and hence immoral, not only to hide a truth so deep and important but also to attack the very source of so many of our deepest and most important truths.

Thus for progressives as well, an attack on truth is an attack on freedom—in this case freedom of inquiry.

On the Web site of the Discovery Institute are some remarkable claims. Not just the claim that intelligent design as a theory is just as good as evolution, but rather that there is evidence from scientific investigation itself in favor of intelligent design! As a cognitive scientist, I am quite interested in what counts as such "evidence."

What the authors did was take metaphorical descriptions of scientific results, pick out all the metaphors that describe events as the results of actions, then take the metaphors as literally true: Every action, in this reading, necessarily implies an actor. For example, consider an article that describes DNA metaphorically as having messages encoded in it. If it's "encoded," there must be an encoder. Or a paper that describes the complex structure of the cell. Well, if it's complex, it must be put together out of simpler elements. And if it's "put together," someone must have put it together. If there are "information-rich genes," then someone must have put the information there, and if there's "information," someone must be doing the informing. If there are "highly organized physical organizations," then someone had to do the organizing. Metaphors are read as if they are literal truths. And not just *any* literal truths. In each case, a complex system involving complex causation is described using verbs of direct causation: "encode," "put together," "inform," "organize."

Advocates of intelligent design seem to have no idea of what real science is. Real science requires evidence—converging evidence. In evolution, there is massive converging evidence: Millions of fossils with carbon 14 dating have to fit together into a time line. That evidence has to converge with the geological evidence from all the places where the fossils were found. And the fossil and geological evidence has to converge with the DNA evidence. That's what makes evolution the most overwhelmingly supported science there is.

These are facts, millions of them fitting together. But they do not fit the fundamentalists' frame. When the facts don't fit the frame, the frame stays and the facts are ignored.

THE LANGUAGE

Now that we have worked though the logic behind the politics of fundamentalist Christianity, let us take a look at the language. Stem-cell research is an excellent example of the fundamentalist use of language. The conservative language technicians suggested that this scientific technique always be referred to as "*embryonic* stem-cell research" since the word "embryo" evokes the conventional image of a little baby. Actually, stem-cell research is carried out on blastocysts—hollow spheres about five days old consisting only of stem cells. As Arnold Kriegstein, director of the Developmental and Stem Cell Biology Program at the University of California's San Francisco School of Medicine, said in a *Dallas Morning News* interview, "In the stage used—a 3- to 5-day-old embryo—there are no distinct organs. There aren't even cells that could be categorized as bone or skin," just undifferentiated stem cells in a hollow sphere. Yet former Republican leader of the House, Tom DeLay, referred to stem-cell research as the "dismemberment of living, distinct human beings." The word "embryonic" sets the frame, and if the word is allowed to stand, it doesn't matter to the public debate what the facts are.

That is an example of surface framing, a single word evoking an image that shifts the discussion in one direction or another. But the repetition of words like "freedom" and "liberty" by the right makes use of deep framing. The logic of the argument begins with the link we described above between truth and freedom:

- The Bible is taken as truth.
- Freedom of speech implies the freedom to speak and communicate the truth.
- Freedom of religion implies the freedom to practice one's religion—to proselytize, to control your children's education, to do charitable works, and to act so as to

follow God's plan by creating a society consistent with fundamentalist Christian values.

Thus, all of their issues are freedom issues: the Pledge of Allegiance, school prayer, abortion, gay marriage, intelligent design, the "war on Christmas," the Ten Commandments, school vouchers, faith-based programs, and so on.

The following passage comes from the Alliance Defense Fund, a legal arm of the Christian right, describing what it does:

> *"Congress shall make no law respecting an establishment of religion, or prohibiting the free exercise thereof . . ."*
>
> The First Amendment of the United States Constitution is unwavering in its affirmation of our religious liberty. Our Founding Fathers knew it was the most basic and inalienable of human rights. It is, in fact, our *First Liberty*.
>
> Founded in 1994 by more than 30 prominent Christian leaders, the Alliance Defense Fund (ADF) was conceived in order to preserve and protect that First Liberty—to defend the right of people of faith to hear and speak the Truth of the Gospel.
>
> Since its inception, ADF has been blessed to see significant progress on the legal landscape. Through the grace of God, legal precedents have been set and much liberty has been reclaimed.

Here we see the link in fundamentalist Christianity between freedom and religion spelled out plainly. "The First Liberty" is "the right of people of faith to hear and speak the Truth of the Gospel." Intelligent design is the truth of the Gospel, which people of faith have the right to hear. Christian prayer in public schools exercises this right. "Under God" in the Pledge of Allegiance exercises this right.

Note that this freedom, this "First Liberty," is a version of what we have called a conservative freedom: It is unconcerned with impinging on the freedoms of others who may not want to hear the "Truth of the Gospel."

Here is the Alliance Defense Fund again:

> The Court explained that it is an undeniable fact that the school district's supervision and control of a high school graduation ceremony places public pressure, as well as peer pressure, on attending students to stand as a group, or at least maintain respectful silence during the invocation and benediction. The Court went on to state, in terms worthy of James Madison, that the Constitution forbids the state to exact religious conformity from a student as the price of attending her own high school graduation . . .
>
> Now, I present this case as Exhibit 1 as an example of what I would call the freedom from religion. Indeed, I would call this an example of freedom from religion taken to its logical extreme . . .
>
> And, thus, this serves as an ideal example of the extreme care with which our legal system now treats the right to be free from any possible imposition of religion upon our lives.

This directive from the Heritage Foundation is an example of fundamentalist freedom of religion:

> Government should protect the religious liberty and integrity of faith-based organizations that participate directly or indirectly in government social service programs. Congress and government agencies should, for example, resist attempts to deny religious organizations the right to use religious belief as a factor in employment decisions.

Here religious freedom consists in the right to discriminate in employment on the basis of religion. It's the same idea as that of the conservative businessman who wants to be able to hire and fire on any discriminatory basis that suits him. But it is more: It is a way to use taxpayer money to support members of a religious denomination—all in the name of "religious liberty."

One of the major claims of fundamentalist Christianity is that religion is the source, and the sole source, of morality, and that fundamentalism is the religion of America. Hence, fundamentalism is the source of morality in America. It follows that their issues are "the moral issues" and their positions on them are *the* moral positions.

They are wrong on all counts. Fundamentalist Christians are a minority of Christians. Traditional American values are progressive. And morality originates outside of religion.

EMPATHY AS THE SOURCE OF MORALITY

Fundamentalists assert that religion is the source of morality. One of the biggest mistakes of the Enlightenment was to counter this claim with the assumption that morality comes from reason. In fact, morality is grounded in empathy, which (as we've already discussed) concerns our biological capacity to connect emotionally with others, to feel how they feel.

Remember that we come prewired with neural connections linking the premotor cortex (which "choreographs" complex actions) and the parietal cortex (which integrates perceptual information). These connections contain mirror neurons that fire when you either perform a complex action or see someone else performing the same action.

This area of the brain has connections to emotional regions. When you see another person's face and body registering the physiological correlates of emotions, your own mirror neurons are activated, and via connections to emotion regions, you can feel what someone else appears to be feeling.

The mirror neurons are believed to be "tuned" in childhood, as a result of positive nurturant parent-child interactions called "attachment." A failure to cultivate empathy in a child can lead to a failure in the child to feel it.

Morality is ultimately about recognizing and responding to others' needs—it is about empathy. Morality therefore arises and develops independent of religion. It comes to religion second-hand.

Religion does not have any special claim to morality. Nor does radical conservatism. At this writing, only 12.7 percent of Americans claim to be evangelical Protestants—and many evangelicals, like Jimmy Carter, are progressives. Most Christians are progressive.

Progressives in general must articulate their views in moral terms, which is not the "shift to the right" that some are calling for. Progressives need to make explicit what is already inherent in their worldview—vigorous ideas about virtue, morality, character, and freedom embodied in its central value, empathy.

And progressive evangelicals have a special mission. They are being misrepresented as fundamentalists. Jesus was a progressive, and to follow in his footsteps is to live progressive values. That's the good news!

11

FOREIGN POLICY AND FREEDOM

George W. Bush has made foreign policy the centerpiece of his presidency. And he has made it relentlessly clear, in speech after speech, that the focus of his presidency is defending and spreading freedom. Yet progressives see in Bush's policies not freedom but outrages against freedom.

They are indeed outrages against the traditional American ideal of freedom—progressive freedom. It is not the American ideal of freedom to invade countries that don't threaten us, to torture people and defend the practice, to jail people indefinitely without due process, and to spy on our own citizens without a warrant.

But it is self-deception to think that Bush does not have a radical conservative view of "freedom" that indeed makes these outrages instances of "freedom" from his point of view.

There are two opposed views of freedom in our nation: strict and nurturant. As we have seen, strict father morality unifies the right's conception of personal, economic, and religious freedom. Strict father morality defines freedom in Bush's foreign policy, tying it in surprising ways to his domestic agenda.

WHY?

Why did Bush speak of an "axis of evil" that linked three very different countries, Iraq, Iran, and North Korea?

Strict father morality sees evil as a strong, tangible force in the world. There is a clear and strict good-evil dichotomy and the need for an overpoweringly strong strict father (who is inherently good) to protect against evil. This carefully chosen phrase echoed Ronald Reagan's calling the Soviet Union the "evil empire." A fight against evil itself justifies spending as much as necessary. It justifies cutting social programs. The phrase also echoes the Axis powers of World War II, identifying those three nations as a kind of alliance held together by their evil essence. It is hard to justify not opposing "evil." Evil poses a threat of harm and coercion, and hence a threat to freedom.

Why, instead of following Colin Powell's suggestion to treat the September 11 attack as a crime, did Bush declare a "war on terror"?

Fear activates and reinforces the strict father model. The war on terror metaphor is used, first, to frighten and intimidate the American public; second, to centralize Bush's war powers in the executive branch and enhance his role as commander in chief; and third, to allow him to run the country as if it were the military, which is a strict father organization in which morality is obedience to orders.

Since there will never be a time when there will be no terrorism or its potential, a war on terror can go on without end, the president's war powers can extend indefinitely, and a permanent strict father approach to government, both at home and abroad, is given legitimacy, especially in foreign policy. The pretext is a defense of freedom.

Why did the Bush administration use and try to justify torture?

If, as strict father morality tells us, the president is fighting evil itself, then he can justify using the devil's own means against him in protecting the nation. Acts that might seem evil otherwise, are just matters of self-defense, a defense of freedom.

Torture? We need the information to prevent a possible attack to protect Americans' freedom, because, after all, terrorists attacked us "because they hate our freedom."

You suspect that someone might have such information? Arrest him and hold him without due process.

You need the information to prevent the possibility of attack? Use torture.

Congress passes a law against it? Overrule Congress.

The Constitution says you can't? Overrule the Constitution. Appoint judges to the Supreme Court who will back you up.

The Geneva conventions guarantee rights of captives? The president's need to fight evil overrides the Geneva conventions.

Spying on American citizens? Some of them might be terrorists or might have information about an attack. Just in case, we'd better spy. To spy on Americans, the FISA law says you need a warrant. It's easy to get if you have any good reason at all. A request takes a few minutes and is almost never turned down. But the president is commander in chief. He has war powers and, in his view, they override any considerations, FISA law or no FISA law. The president has to assert his authority under those war powers or he might lose that authority. Besides, it would be immoral not to. The strict father is the ultimate moral authority, and it is his moral duty to assert that authority. The president morally should not obey the FISA law in a state of war—or admit any higher authority!

And what constitutes "terrorism"? Strict father morality gives the strict father, who knows right from wrong and is unquestionably good, the authority to decide. The Bush administration has decided that certain purely domestic acts against property in the name of environmental or animal rights activism (for example, releasing minks from mink farms or setting afire SUVs on new car lots) constitute acts of "terrorism." The Patriot Act supersedes laws protecting the rights of citizens. It allows the arrest of suspected activists, enacts harsh penalties for "terrorism," and justifies spying on environmental and animal rights activists, now renamed "terrorists"! In other words, defending property rights is now "defending freedom" against all enemies, foreign and domestic. Declaring a war on terror has given Bush, at least as he sees it, expansive war powers that can be extended for the length of his presidency—in the name of freedom.

What has determined Bush's attitude toward the United Nations, the World Court, international treaties (such as the nuclear test ban treaty), and our allies France and Germany?

One of the central metaphors of American foreign policy is that of the nation-as-person in a world community, where there are neighborhoods and neighbors, friendly states, enemy states, and rogue states. In this metaphor, there are adult and child states. The industrialized states are the grown-ups and the developing and underdeveloped nations are the children.

In the strict father model, the adults tell the children what to do, and if they don't do it, they are punished, say, with "fiscal discipline" or military intervention. A "police action" suggests intervening to enforce obedience to the law—of the adult states. In this metaphor, it is in the interest of a person to be strong, healthy, and influential, so it is in the national interest to be militarily strong, economically healthy, and politically influential.

The United States is the most industrialized and most powerful nation, and it assumes it knows right from wrong and acts morally—indeed, that it is a moral paragon in the world that knows inherently how other countries should be run. Its essence at its founding was to be good. It is the very model of a strict father. The strict father is the leader of the family, both the strongest person and the moral authority. So, in the world community, which consists mostly of developing and underdeveloped nations, the United States is the moral authority, and it enforces this authority through strength, through military and financial power.

This is not old-school realpolitik, maximizing self-interest and no more. Force is used in the name of good and freedom from evil and oppression. The self-interest of the United States is, in this view, for the good of the world. Our self-interest is theirs too. It is classic "this may hurt but it's for your own good" strict father logic.

Just as the strict father should never give up his authority in the family, so the United States should never abandon its sovereignty in the world. Not to the UN. Not to its closest allies. Not to the World Court. Even if it means opting out of treaty obligations.

Just as the strict father enforces his judgment with force, so should the United States.

Just as the strict father should act in advance to prevent children from becoming rebellious and challenging his authority, so the United States should strike preemptively to prevent other nations from challenging the hegemony of the United States.

Just as the strict father acts benignly for the benefit of all, so the United States acts benignly for the sake of peace and freedom. Our allies should recognize this.

During the occupation of Iraq, the United States has run the country, determined which Iraqis could have governing power and, to a large extent, what the Iraqi constitution could say. How is this seen as "freedom" for the Iraqis?

Just as children first have to be under the discipline of the father and learn right from wrong, then learn internal discipline, so the Iraqis must first be ruled by the United States and be told how to write a Constitution, then learn how to gain the internal discipline to govern themselves. And just as a child newly reaching adulthood will make mistakes, so will a new democracy like Iraq.

As President Bush said in his second inaugural: "Self-government relies, in the end, on the government of the self." The government of the self is the internal discipline required to be moral. Applied to Iraq, this means that Iraqi democracy (self-government) requires an Iraqi governing force that maintains legitimate order inside Iraq (the government of the self). The Iraqis must learn internal discipline just as a child must. And the father may withdraw the threat of punishment—bring the troops home—only when self-discipline is achieved.

NEOCONSERVATIVE DEMOCRATIC THEORY

As we have seen, in the conservative view, the unfettered free market is the mechanism that permits moral discipline to result in prosperity. So large corporations, wealthy stockholders, and landholders rightfully assume governing power. The free-market freedom theory says that free trade (the introduction of "free markets" globally) will necessarily result in the spread of democracy. Here is an outline of that theory.

FREE-MARKET FREEDOM

Large corporations and wealthy investors and landholders need to protect themselves, their profits, and their property. To do so, they will insist on certain protections, and because of the influence of their wealth, they can get them instituted:

- Relatively free elections: protect their property from dictators and corrupt politicians
- Civilian control of the military: protects them and their property from military coups
- Balance of power among branches of government: protects their property from dangerous concentrations of political power

- Civil liberties: protects them and their property from police power
- Free press: unearths abuses of power in government and provides access to information needed for business

A necessary assumption of this view of democracy is the benevolent influence of large corporations and the wealthy. It is a kind of trickle-down democracy—democracy for large corporations and the wealthy eventually means democracy for everyone else.

President Bush often equates free markets and political freedom:

> Trade and Markets are freedom.
> —quoted in Howard Fischer,
> "Bush Places Free Trade Above Land, Labor
> Issues," *Arizona Daily Star*, December 8, 1999

> From the recent history of the Asia Pacific region, we know that freedom is indivisible. The economic liberty that builds prosperity also builds a demand for limited government and self-rule. Modernization and progress eventually require freedom in all its forms. And the advance of freedom is good for all, because free societies are peaceful societies.
> —radio address to the nation, November 20, 2004

Bush is invoking the economic freedom of the economic liberty myth together with the political freedom of the free-market freedom theory.

Here is Colin Powell, speaking at the Heritage Foundation on December 12, 2002, building support for the invasion of Iraq and proposing a "U.S.–Middle East Partnership Initiative."

> The spread of democracy and free markets, fueled by the wonders of the technological revolution, has created a dy-

namo that can generate prosperity and human well-being on an unprecedented scale. But this revolution has largely left the Middle East behind . . . Internally, many economies are stifled by regulation and cronyism. They lack transparency and are closed to entrepreneurship, investment, and trade . . . Combined with rigid political systems, it is a dangerous brew indeed. Along with freer economies, many of the peoples of the Middle East need a stronger political voice. We reject the condescending notion that freedom will not grow in the Middle East or that there is any region of the world that cannot support democracy . . . Given a choice between tyranny and freedom, people choose freedom . . .

Our initiative rests on three pillars. We will engage with public and private-sector groups to bridge the jobs gap with economic reform, business investment, and private-sector development. We will partner with community leaders to close the freedom gap with projects to strengthen civil society, expand political participation, and lift the voices of women. And we will work with parents and educators to bridge the knowledge gap with better schools and more opportunities for higher education.

Ladies and gentlemen, hope begins with a paycheck . . . we will work with governments to establish economic rules and regulations that will attract foreign investment and allow the private sector to flourish.

Powell is presenting classic free-market freedom: Strict father economics leads to democracy.

Free-market freedom explains the attitude of the Bush administration toward recent political developments in Venezuela, Bolivia, Brazil, and Chile, where leaders have been elected who openly oppose laissez-faire free markets as not benefiting large impoverished segments of their populations. As you might expect, the Bush administration does not see these democratically elected governments in a positive light. Rather, it sees these changes as movements away from freedom and democracy, movements that threaten freedom—that is, free-market freedom—in the world.

But beyond free-market freedom, there is an even stronger neoconservative vision. We can see this in the Bush administration's inaccurate predictions about the Iraq War, predictions born of ideology, not evidence.

Why did the neoconservatives predict that simply toppling Saddam would bring democracy? Why did they think that American troops would be greeted with rose petals? Why did they stage Bush's now-embarrassing "Mission Accomplished" landing on the aircraft carrier as the troops marched into Baghdad?

General Eric Shinseki had estimated that several hundred thousand American troops would be necessary to bring order to Iraq. Donald Rumsfeld overruled him—and fired him as head of the Joint Chiefs of Staff—sending only one-fourth to one-third as many troops. Shinseki was right. Why was Rumsfeld so wrong?

Reasoning within the strict father model leads to a preference for thinking in terms of direct causation, not systemic causation. Direct causal reasoning says you free a country by removing the tyrant. That all that's necessary: simple direct causation. "Regime change" is all that's needed. The troops march in, the statue of Saddam comes down, and it's all over. The fall of one person will automatically lead to freedom, democracy, an ordered civil society, and economic prosperity.

In addition, there was a second, implicit neoconservative theory of democracy—a natural accompaniment to free-market freedom. Let's call it self-interest democracy. If it sounds familiar, it should. Radical conservatives see big government as tyranny, and they view the removal of tyrants as similar to shrinking big government and drowning it in a bathtub. Here is self-interest democracy:

- Everyone is, and should be, motivated primarily by self-interest.
- If everyone is free to pursue his or her self-interest, then the interests of all will be maximized, as a law of nature, by the invisible hand.
- Democracy is the system of government that permits this.
- Tyranny keeps people from pursuing their own interests; the tyrant's interests prevail.
- All you have to do is remove the tyrant, and democracy is inevitable. Just as all you have to do is shrink government—eliminate regulation, taxes, class action suits, and social programs—and economic prosperity will prevail.

You don't need several hundred thousand troops. One-quarter of that was enough to remove Saddam. After that, everything should have been hunky-dory, if not right away, then not long afterward.

The idea of self-interest democracy makes some sense of Donald Rumsfeld's classic comment on the lawlessness, chaos, and looting that accompanied the "liberation" of Iraq: "Stuff happens, and it's untidy, and freedom's untidy, and free people are free to make mistakes and commit crimes and do bad things." Freedom from the tyrant produces an immediate stew of self-interest, including looting and lawbreaking, but when it settles down—to self-interest driven by discipline—democracy will prevail.

Perhaps not enough time has passed, but so far the predictions have not been met. What has gone wrong?

On the whole, strict father reasoning has failed.

First, direct causation failed. Iraq is a very complex system: twenty-five million people, three major religious and ethnic divisions, hatreds and blood feuds for generations, a history of violence, and no experience of democracy. The country was cobbled together by the British from remnants of the Ottoman Empire. It never had a national identity. Systemic causation prevails. Saddam's brutality was holding the country together. When that was removed, all hell broke loose—the old religious and ethnic hatreds were realized in violence, and without several hundred thousand troops, there could be no order.

Second, self-interest democracy makes the mistake of essentialism: It assumes everyone is the same and by nature motivated primarily by self-interest. One of the many problems with this assumption is that it does not take into account the existence of suicide bombers, who operate not from self-interest but from love for and utter devotion to God, as well as vengeance against an enemy that has, in their view, humiliated their culture and their faith.

Third, free-market freedom ignores the use of the common wealth for the common good through the building of the infrastructure. Iraq had virtually no functioning infrastructure. Saddam put his money elsewhere, allowing what there was to fall into disrepair, and between American bombing attacks and more than a decade of embargoes, the rest was destroyed and not replaced. So-called free markets cannot function without such infrastructure: roads, bridges, transportation systems, electric lines, communication systems, hospitals, sewage systems, a police force, and industrial infrastructure like functioning oil refineries. Three years after the invasion and occupation, two basics of common wealth infrastructure still have not been established: electricity and security.

Free-market freedom also requires jobs. No electricity, no security, no jobs! And the most lucrative rebuilding contracts went to American corporations like Halliburton. Partly for fear of sabotage and partly for the maximization of American corporate profits, jobs are being outsourced to Americans—not because Americans are paid less, but because Americans are paid more.

RELIGION AND FOREIGN POLICY

For President Bush, fundamentalist Christianity ultimately supports a moral foreign policy and economic policy:

> A religion that demands individual moral accountability, and encourages the encounter of the individual with God, is fully compatible with the rights and responsibilities of self-government.
>
> —speech presented at the twentieth anniversary of the National Endowment for Democracy, November 6, 2003

Individual moral accountability is what is demanded of the child in the strict father family and by God in fundamentalist religion. Individual responsibility is the moral touchstone of right-wing politics. And it is the basis of strict father economics, in which government should provide nothing for the individual, who is on his own and completely responsible for himself, requiring no support from community or country. Free-market freedom leads inevitably to democracy and to right-wing "freedoms" in all domains of life. Religion, economics, family values, and foreign policy are one. Human rights in other countries—which the United States all too often has authority to impose—are taken to include unrestricted free markets, free trade, and the freedom of fundamentalist Christians to practice and proselytize, to be free to speak their "truth."

Accordingly, Christian missionaries are seen as exercising a "human right" when they attempt to convert indigenous people to Christianity, and any restrictions on missionaries are seen as "antidemocratic" and an affront to human rights. Accordingly, it is taken as appropriate that fundamentalist Christian beliefs guide important aspects of American foreign policy. One of George Bush's first acts in office was to stop American aid to all reproductive health clinics that performed abortions or even counseled women on how to obtain safe abortions. The Bush administration agrees with the pope: The essence of woman is to bear children. Family planning and reproductive health clinics should therefore not be part of American foreign policy.

But this is the least of the commonality between fundamentalist religion and Bush's foreign policy. Evangelical fundamentalism is about spreading the "good news," about being a missionary and having a mission. That religious mission is about freedom, as we saw in Chapter 10: how to become free of sin and free of hell and suffering for all eternity. Strict father Christianity is the answer. First, take Jesus as Savior, and have all your previous sins washed away. Second, follow God's commandments, following the path of Jesus, and you will be saved from eternal suffering in hell. Third, it is your mission to pass the word on.

Bush has a mission as well: to spread the radical conservative version of freedom and democracy, and its foundation, strict father morality, which is identical to the foundation of fundamentalist religion. The fundamentalist mission fits the neoconservative mission. Bush, as a thoroughgoing radical conservative—fundamentalist *and* neoconservative—has two missions at once. Both concern the spread of "freedom."

THE NATIONAL INTEREST

In our discussion of the nation-as-person metaphor, we saw that just as it is in the interest of a person to be strong, healthy, and influential, so it is in the national interest for the nation as a whole to be militarily strong, economically healthy, and politically influential. That is what the national interest is about—not about individual people, who may be impoverished, in debt, disabled, aged, uneducated, sick, or discriminated against. If the

GDP and the stock market are up, the military is strong, and the country can intimidate other nations and twist arms around the world, the national interest is served.

THE DEMOCRATIC IDEAL

From the time America broke free of England in the American Revolution, freedom has been a centerpiece in American foreign policy. The goals have been what we will call the democratic ideal:

- To protect our domestic freedoms
- To extend those freedoms to other nations

Besides defending our freedoms from foreign conquest, it became a goal of our foreign policy to be a "beacon of freedom to the world," to be a "shining City on a Hill"—an example to the world of the possibilities of a free society.

All too often our national interest has been at odds with our freedom-loving ideals. We supported dictatorships when they served our national interest. We even supported Saddam Hussein once as a buffer against Iran, and we now support Saudi Arabia.

For this reason, it was notable when George W. Bush, defending his Iraq War policy, said in his second inaugural address, "America's vital interests and our deepest beliefs are now one." He might have meant, "We pursue our national interest independent of our democratic ideals, but in Iraq they happen to coincide." But I think his remark had a deeper meaning.

- In strict father morality, pursuing self-interest *is* being moral.

- In the democratic ideal, being moral ("our deepest beliefs") *is* bringing about freedom and democracy (via free-market freedom).

Suppose we pursue the following foreign policy (Neoconservatism):

- Build up and use our military strength (military self-interest)
- to impose free-market freedom (economic self-interest),
- thus creating a democracy and a democratic ally (political self-interest).

In this foreign policy, pursuing the national interest *is* achieving the democratic ideal. This is the Bush Middle East policy and the neoconservative rationale behind the Iraq War.

To repeat, "America's vital interests and our deepest beliefs are now one." The line takes on a new meaning: America's foreign policy, as exemplified in the Iraq War, is at once supremely moral and pragmatic. The plan was this: American geopolitical interests in Iraq—oil, military supremacy in the region, Israeli security, and political leverage—were to be pursued by using our military to impose a free-market democracy in Iraq, a system that is essentially moral, embracing freedom both in Iraq and in the homeland, now protected from terrorists. It's idealistic: Iraq is free and democratic, we remain free and protected, Israel is protected. And it's self-interest: We control the oil, we are the supreme military power in the region, and we have political leverage. "America's vital interests and our deepest beliefs are now one."

The plan was drawn up long before September 11, 2001.

THE PROJECT FOR A NEW
AMERICAN CENTURY

George W. Bush's foreign policy was designed before he took office and was described in a document issued on June 3, 1997, by a group called the Project for a New American Century. The signers included a number of the most influential guides to foreign policy in the later Bush administration: Dick Cheney, I. Lewis Libby, Donald Rumsfeld, and Paul Wolfowitz, as well as the president's brother Jeb Bush and the president's father's vice president, Dan Quayle. The signers also included many of the right wing's leading intellectuals—William J. Bennett, Midge Decter, Francis Fukuyama, Donald Kagan, and Norman Podhoretz—as well such power brokers as Elliott Abrams, Gary Bauer, and Steve Forbes. The statement of principles included the following:

> If we shirk our responsibilities, we invite challenges to our fundamental interests. The history of the 20th century should have taught us that it is important to shape circumstances before crises emerge, and to meet threats before they become dire. The history of this century should have taught us to embrace the cause of American leadership.
>
> Our aim is to remind Americans of these lessons and to draw their consequences for today. Here are four consequences:
>
> - we need to increase defense spending significantly if we are to carry out our global responsibilities today and modernize our armed forces for the future;
> - we need to strengthen our ties to democratic allies and to challenge regimes hostile to our interests and values;

- we need to promote the cause of political and economic freedom abroad;
- we need to accept responsibility for America's unique role in preserving and extending an international order friendly to our security, our prosperity, and our principles.

In 1998, PNAC wrote and published an open letter to President Clinton proposing an invasion of Iraq. This was to become the basis of the Bush foreign policy and the framework for Bush's claim to be promoting freedom in the world.

The strict father must at all times maintain his moral authority and make sure it is not challenged by unruly children. As soon as the children get out of hand, he must use preemptive force to keep them in line. He has a unique responsibility to teach them right from wrong, to get them to internalize the principles of what's right and what's wrong. If he teaches them correctly, then he can depend upon their knowledge and their discipline to be sure they do what is right and not what is wrong, so that they can be prosperous and free.

As the strict father is leader in the family, so the president is leader of the country, and America is leader of the world. Being the "leader" means that he (1) is the moral authority who knows right from wrong, is inherently good, and can be trusted to do what is right; (2) has, and must use, great power to do right; (3) is responsible for protecting us from evildoers and may have to use preemptive force; (4) has the authority to do whatever is necessary; (5) requires obedience from followers (who he is protecting); (6) may have to fight fire with fire as part of protection; (7) pursues his self-interest, which is in the interest of everyone; and (8) serves the prosperity and freedom of all. Strict father morality maps directly onto PNAC principles, which describe the Bush foreign policy.

PROGRESSIVE VERSUS CONSERVATIVE FOREIGN POLICY

We can now understand radical conservatives' views on a wide range of diverse foreign policy issues. Radical conservatives look down on the UN, don't accept the authority of the World Court, and see international organizations as impinging on American sovereignty, our essential goodness. They approve of preemptive war. They want free trade without environmental, labor, or social regulations, and with maximal privatization. They view war and the dangerous expansion of executive power as appropriate responses to terrorism. They want to maintain a world oil economy and are against introducing environmental regulations into world affairs.

Progressives—at least the idealists among them—have exactly the opposite views on all these matters. Why? What brings progressives together on these foreign policy positions? And what do the answers have to do with different understandings of freedom?

BILL CLINTON'S PRAGMATISM

Progressive foreign policy has always had the dual democratic ideals of protecting our freedoms and extending them to others—where freedom is understood from a progressive perspective. During the Cold War, the ideal of extending freedom was overridden by "realism"—advancing our national interest in the military, economic, and political spheres, even when it meant dealing with dictators or closing our eyes to political oppression and even genocide.

During the Clinton administration, a transition began. President Clinton at first refused to interfere in the Rwandan genocide since it was not in our vital national interest, and later regretted it for moral reasons, as he began to see the national interest served by moral action. Where George H. W. Bush refused to intervene in Bosnia, citing a lack of vital interests there (no oil), Clinton did use the American military in Bosnia and Kosovo, deciding that democratic idealism (stopping ethnic cleansing, extending freedom to others) did, in itself, serve our national interest. Indeed, there was a redefinition of the national interest under Clinton; for example, he attempted to add labor rights and environmental regulations to trade agreements—a form of democratic idealism: bringing our freedoms to other nations. The idea was that there would also be a benefit to the United States: Less cheap labor abroad competing with our labor force would take fewer jobs from the United States, thus helping American labor. Radical conservatives thwarted such progressive moves on labor and the environment.

The Clinton approach had two parts: Clinton made a shift in the traditional priorities defining the national interest, giving priority to economics and diplomacy over the military whenever possible. Given this, Clinton took a pragmatic approach: Pursue the ideals, but only insofar as a case could be made that they independently served the national interest as he had redefined it to stress economics and diplomacy over the use of the military whenever possible, except for peacekeeping missions.

This approach flew in the face of neoconservatives. The PNAC response to Clinton's policies was predictable:

> Cuts in foreign affairs and defense spending, inattention to the tools of statecraft, and inconstant leadership are making it increasingly difficult to sustain American influence around the world. And the promise of short-term commercial benefits threatens to override strategic considerations.

Clinton had been educated in "realist" Cold War policies and considered himself a centrist. In addition, he had to deal with a radically conservative Republican Congress. Nonetheless, he made moves in the direction of progressive idealism.

PROGRESSIVE IDEALISM

One can best understand the progressive approach to foreign policy by looking at it in its purest form: progressive idealism, where the democratic ideal (protecting our freedoms and extending them to others) defines the national interest. Protecting our freedoms means real protection from terrorism, and a lot more: protection of workers, consumers, and the environment built into trade agreements; protecting jobs by minimizing outsourcing; protecting civil liberties.

To see what it means to export our freedoms to other countries, let us start at the center of progressive thought—empathy and responsibility—with the implied values of protection, fairness, fulfillment, opportunity, community, and trust. In foreign policy, empathy means empathizing with people of other nations—with individual citizens, not with states. It means wanting those in other countries to have the progressive freedoms we either have or are pursuing here.

Many of the world's most urgent problems are not now considered part of foreign policy at all, because they are below the level of the state. Yet those issues persist with greater and greater urgency around the world: women's rights, children's rights, refugee issues, labor rights, public health, and, of course, hunger and poverty. Empathy and responsibility, the central progressive values, turn these global problems into foreign policy problems as part of extending our progressive freedoms to the world.

A good example is freedom for women: the freedom to vote, freedom from forced circumcision, the freedom to have a private sexual life, the freedom to marry who you want to marry, the freedom to pursue an education, the freedom to have a career, the freedom to function in public as men do—drive a car, wear the clothes you want, etc. This is usually not considered part of foreign policy. But for progressives it is part of what foreign policy needs to be.

Extending progressive freedoms to others means changing foreign policy drastically—looking below the level of the state, in case after case. Freedom for working people means freedom from cheap labor traps, freedom from inhuman working conditions, freedom to get an education, freedom to get capital to start a small business. Extending our freedoms abroad means bringing into foreign policy issues like hunger and poverty, the global environment, refugee horrors, world health—issues tackled by international agencies, some associated with the UN. Working with international agencies and the UN and helping to make those institutions more effective in these areas become foreign policy responsibilities.

Here is what progressive foreign policy, based on an empathy-and-responsibility perspective on morality, entails:

Avoiding war whenever possible—removing war as an instrument of policy. In war, enormous numbers of noncombatants—women, children, and the aged—get killed and maimed. Families are destroyed, homes are destroyed, infrastructure is destroyed, with disastrous consequences for individuals, especially the poor.

War must be an absolute last resort. This means maximizing the use of diplomatic and economic solutions. It also means rethinking the military—keeping war as an option but redirecting the military to peacekeeping and disaster relief.

Torture must be outlawed and eliminated. Even on pragmatic grounds, it does not yield reliable intelligence, and it is morally abhorrent.

International treaties, such as the nuclear test ban treaty, should be honored and extended. Nuclear weapons development should end; the use of *any* nuclear weapons is unthinkably dangerous. The use of so-called depleted uranium should end. It is misnamed; its radioactivity is not "depleted." It is still radioactive. Its use is ubiquitous in the U.S. military. It poisons our own troops, and used shells are left all over Iraq, poisoning the people we are supposedly freeing.

Private contractors should not take over military functions; they have no accountability for what they do. The National Guard should not be used to fight wars abroad; they are not properly trained, are needed at home, and did not sign up for such duty.

The empathy and responsibility that extend our freedom to others turn free trade into fair trade: avoiding cheap labor traps abroad, preserving indigenous ways of life, preserving nature, preventing monocultures, greatly limiting the power of transnational corporations to govern the lives of people in the third world, keeping clean water freely available, preventing the theft of the mineral wealth of a country so that a fair share goes to the people of that country—in short, maximizing for others the everyday freedoms we either enjoy or seek for ourselves, while also maximizing the benefits of trade.

Trade issues have been inhibiting our ability to extend our freedoms to others. Internet companies like Yahoo and AOL are helping the Chinese to censor Internet content and are even turning over the names of people engaged in "subversive" online activity. The cost of doing business is supporting the suppression of free speech. Our government should be supporting American companies in resisting such suppression, instead of using the same means to spy on our own citizens.

Terrorism should be seen in terms of crime, not war, and fought in the most positive and least violent way. The war in Iraq increased terrorism by creating new terrorists. To work against Islamic terrorism, we should be supporting extensive networks of moderate Islamic schools to replace madrasas. Indeed, there should be overwhelming support for the development and popularization of moderate Islam. The financial support coming from Saudi Arabia should be cut off. The intelligence agencies need to hire more Arabic speakers. Arabic should be taught widely in this country and there should be cultural missions to Islamic countries.

Empathy and responsibility extend not just to other individuals, or just to human beings, but further to the earth itself as a biological system and all the living things on it. This means, among other things, recognizing the reality of global warming, perhaps the greatest threat to the earth as we know it. We should be working with other countries to cut down on the use of fossil fuels and should put in place a massive program to develop alternative energy sources. Such a program would have important foreign policy consequences. It would vastly reduce our dependence on Middle East oil. New energy technologies could be marketed, or given away, to developing countries; they would then not have to buy oil, or borrow the money to buy oil, or clean up the mess from using oil. Because clean energy is available everywhere, every country has the potential to be an energy producer, not a consumer.

The cost to our country of maintaining an oil-based economy has been enormous—not just the cost of the oil itself but also the cost in lives lost, in bodies maimed, and in money misspent. Dependence on oil must end.

Defending our freedoms requires real homeland security; under Bush, a vast amount has been spent with little effect. Our ports, railways, and chemical plants are not safe. Hurricane Katrina showed that we are not prepared for disasters, natural or otherwise. This lack of preparedness is a matter of radical conservative policy: Defund agencies like FEMA that function for the public good; hire private industry; use the military; ignore the needs of people impoverished by disaster, who, if they had been disciplined enough, would be okay and who have only themselves to blame if they're not. This attitude is despicable. We must rethink homeland security seriously from a progressive perspective, correcting all the conservative defects in the policy.

We do not defend our freedoms by giving up our freedoms. At Bush's directive, intelligence agencies have been spying on our citizens without warrants. We have been jailing people without charges or due process. This must end. The defense and spread of conservative freedom is the death of progressive, traditional American freedom.

PART IV

IDEAS AND ACTION

12

BUSH'S "FREEDOM"

Bush's second inaugural address was a work of rhetorical art. More than half of the time, the use of "freedom," "free," and "liberty" was in a context neutral enough to fit the simple, uncontested sense—or either the progressive or conservative senses. The words could mean whatever one wanted them to mean, depending on one's political leanings. Many of Bush's phrases could have been said by a Democrat with the opposite policies.

Sentence by sentence, they sounded like traditional patriotic language. Even a liberal as sophisticated as Elaine Kamarck was taken in. But Bush was speaking in the context of defending his controversial policies. This made it seem as if his policies fit the traditional sense of freedom—which, as we have seen, they clearly do not.

While much of the time Bush was using a vague idea of freedom, he also made specific references to right-wing freedom, evoking the frames of the radical conservatives. There is the reference to "the force of human freedom," linking freedom to the use of force. He warns us that freedom faces a dangerous threat: The "survival of liberty" reinforces his claim that the Iraq War is part of a war for our survival. The use of "liberty" within the American context is an appeal to conservative populists and an inherent attack on liberals who criticize the war and, in Bush's view, threaten our survival. The "survival of liberty" also evokes the idea that liberals who oppose the war are enemies of America.

The association of democracy and freedom with fundamentalist Christianity and creationism is made by reference to "the Maker of Heaven and earth," followed up by "the imperative of self-government," where "imperative" suggests obedience to God's commandments. The fundamentalist battle of good against evil is echoed in "life is fragile, and evil is real . . ."

Right-wing economic freedom and the economic liberty myth are evoked in the section implicitly attacking Social Security through reference to "the ownership society." The curious phrase "preparing our people for the challenges of life in a free society" suggests that we are now economic slaves to the government, implicitly echoes the right-wing cry for "economic freedom," and touches on the theme that discipline is required for prosperity. The right-wing idea that only the disciplined deserve prosperity and the freedom it brings is reinforced by the use of the code word "character": "the public interest depends on private character." The suggestion is that liberal elites are destroying the fabric of morality in America. Then, the heart of strict father morality: "Self-government relies, in the end, on the government of the self," as we discussed. Neoconservative missionary foreign policy is then telegraphed in the important sentence "America's vital interests and our deepest beliefs are now one." And, nearing the end, creationism is tied to patriotism by invoking "the Author of Liberty."

There are mostly uncontested uses of "freedom" and "liberty" in support, via context, of a highly contested policy, sprinkled through with the full range of right-wing uses of "freedom" and "liberty." The effect is to help commandeer both the word and the idea.

Here is the context. Bush has just been reelected, running on his post-9/11 record and the war in Iraq as the person most likely to defend the country against terrorist attack. But it has come

out, through leaks from former insiders, that he intended to attack Iraq from the first week he came into office. No weapons of
mass destruction were found, and it appears that intelligence was
doctored or twisted in order to marshal support for the war. Democrats have called the war one of "choice," not "necessity."

> At this second gathering, our duties are defined not by the
> words I use, but by the history we have seen together.

"The history we have seen together" is 9/11 and the events that
followed. But the words he uses are intended to reframe the context: These events defined certain duties for us, which we ignore
at our peril. His "duties" include assuming war powers (extraordinary authority given to this president) and going to war in Iraq.
The claim is that those war powers are "duties" thrust upon him
by external events beyond his control, rather than powers assumed by fiat. "The history we have seen together" suggests a
common knowledge and understanding of events, while in fact
the reverse is true—the account of events is considerably contested.

> For a half century, America defended our own freedom by
> standing watch on distant borders.

This ignores the Vietnam War, our experience closest to the Iraq
War, where we were driven out of the country with huge losses.

> After the shipwreck of communism came years of relative
> quiet, years of repose, years of sabbatical—and then there
> came a day of fire.

The Clinton administration's energetic shift toward the economic over the military, both at home and in diplomacy, is
seen as inaction—"quiet," "repose," "sabbatical"—leaving be-

hind one's duties and work, as if the country were asleep and nothing was happening during the greatest economic boom and period of optimism in our history. Clinton's military containment of Saddam Hussein inside Iraq's no-fly zones, which indeed succeeded in keeping Saddam Hussein from developing weapons of mass destruction, is ignored. The successful uses of the military in Bosnia and Kosovo are also ignored. The idea is that the country was ignoring a gathering military threat. "And then there came a day of fire" refers to 9/11 using the religious language and rhetoric of Revelation:

> We have seen our vulnerability—and we have seen its deepest source. For as long as whole regions of the world simmer in resentment and tyranny—prone to ideologies that feed hatred and excuse murder—violence will gather, and multiply in destructive power, and cross the most defended borders, and raise a mortal threat.

"Simmer" repeats "fire" and suggests that "whole regions of the world" might spark a conflagration. The image is apocalyptic! The ultimate causes are "tyranny" (the absence of democracy) and "resentment" (an echo of "they hate our freedoms" as Bush's explanation of the 9/11 attack). There is no discussion of Osama bin Laden citing the American military bases in Saudi Arabia as a major cause for the attack, and protecting oil interests as a rationale for the Saudi bases. There is no discussion of the Israeli-Palestinian conflict.

> There is only one force of history that can break the reign of hatred and resentment, and expose the pretensions of tyrants, and reward the hopes of the decent and tolerant, and that is the force of human freedom.
>
> We are led, by events and common sense, to one conclusion: The survival of liberty in our land increasingly depends on the success of liberty in other lands. The best

hope for peace in our world is the expansion of freedom in
all the world.

"America's vital interests and our deepest beliefs are now one."

The frame imposed is tyranny versus freedom "in all the
world." We are threatened from around the world. "The survival
of liberty in our land increasingly depends on the success of liberty in other lands . . . the expansion of freedom in all the world."

This is neoconservative foreign policy in missionary language, joined to the traditional "beacon of freedom" idea, although traditionally the "beacon" was planted on our shores and
didn't go out and preemptively attack other countries. This is an
idealist foreign policy, contrasting with the old realist foreign
policy that "contained" tyrants and minimized their effect until
they could be internally overthrown.

Implicit here is the common claim that democracies don't go
to war with other democracies—that if there were democracy
everywhere ("freedom in all the world"), then peace would be realized.

What is not mentioned explicitly is his view, which we have
seen elsewhere, that freedom is free-market freedom, that free
trade is the foothold of free-market freedom and the mechanism
for "the expansion of freedom in all the world." Not mentioned,
but there in context, is his view that the United States has a vital interest in controlling the flow of oil.

That is why "America's vital interests and our deepest beliefs
are now one." In the neoconservative vision, the way to control
the flow of oil in the Middle East and to profit from free trade is
to spread democracy via free-market freedom, when necessary by
the use of force. This is a mission, an evangelical mission.

From the day of our Founding, we have proclaimed that
every man and woman on this earth has rights, and dignity, and matchless value, because they bear the image of
the Maker of Heaven and earth.

Here we have religion intimately tied to democracy. The "Founding" of the country is analogized to the Creation; we are equal not because of the Enlightenment idea that we are equally rational, but rather because we are all made in the image of "the Maker of Heaven and earth"—a description of God that echoes creationism. Patriotism and creationism are one.

> Across the generations we have proclaimed the impera-tive of self-government, because no one is fit to be a mas-ter, and no one deserves to be a slave. Advancing these ideals is the mission that created our Nation. It is the honorable achievement of our fathers. Now it is the ur-gent requirement of our nation's security, and the calling of our time.

The religious overtones continue: "proclaimed the impera-tive . . . the mission that created our Nation . . . the calling . . ." Here is evangelical democracy, modeled on evangelical Chris-tianity, with a mission, a calling. That evangelical mission—spreading democracy—"created our Nation." In other words, it is God's plan for America. But it is more than "advancing . . . ideals"; it is "the urgent requirement of our nation's security." Neoconservatism is evangelical.

At this point, the religious overtones end and language be-comes neutral between progressivism and conservatism for sev-eral paragraphs. Indeed, it sounds like the progressive ideal of protecting our freedoms here and extending them abroad. Here's a typical example:

> All who live in tyranny and hopelessness can know: the United States will not ignore your oppression, or excuse your oppressors. When you stand for your liberty, we will stand with you.

Then the tone shifts: "Today, I also speak anew to my fellow citizens." Here comes the conservative agenda, presented in terms of freedom.

Our country has accepted obligations that are difficult to fulfill, and would be dishonorable to abandon.

Our honor requires that we stay in Iraq despite the fact that the war is going wrong. Read: A moral authority (a political strict father) would lose his authority if he showed weakness. The whole plan of being a moral authority to the world would be shot. How can we expand democracy (that is, free-market freedom) to the whole world if it won't even work in the first place we try? If we leave Iraq, it would shatter the whole neoconservative ideal.

Yet because we have acted in the great liberating tradition of this nation, tens of millions have achieved their freedom.

The Iraqis are already free. Hmmm . . .

Because the war has not been going well—there were not nearly enough soldiers, sent in without adequate training or equipment—recruitment has been off. Getting more recruits is a high administration priority. The frame has been set up so that the Iraq War is not recognized as a choice Bush made well before 9/11, nor as an invasion of a country showing no threat to America, nor as in the interest of American corporations in securing oil. Instead, fighting in Iraq—and perhaps dying or getting maimed for life—is put forth as an ideal, as a sacrifice and a service to one's country ("duty," "allegiance"), rather than as a sacrifice to a neoconservative experiment. Democracy as religion returns: "evil is real . . . serve in a cause . . . larger than yourself, and in your days . . . in a world moving toward liberty . . ." Notice the teleology: The world is inevitably "moving toward liberty." In a fundamentalist context, that is God's plan and it is our job—our duty—to carry it out. Neoconservative foreign policy is a religious mission.

> Some have shown their devotion to our country in deaths that honored their whole lives—and we will always honor their names and their sacrifice.
>
> All Americans have witnessed this idealism, and some for the first time. I ask our youngest citizens to believe the evidence of your eyes. You have seen duty and allegiance in the determined faces of our soldiers. You have seen that life is fragile, and evil is real, and courage triumphs. Make the choice to serve in a cause larger than your wants, larger than yourself—and in your days you will add not just to the wealth of our country, but to its character.
>
> America has need of idealism and courage, because we have essential work at home—the unfinished work of American freedom. In a world moving toward liberty, we are determined to show the meaning and promise of liberty.

"In your days" is religious language. "Add not just to the wealth of our country" refers to America's economic interests. "But to its character" refers to the conservative moral vision, in which character is the internal discipline needed both to be moral and to prosper. The language of American idealism has been merged with the language of conservatism. The metaphor is clear: America is not just a person. America is a conservative! And conservatism is idealistic and serves American ideals.

At this point, the radical conservative economic agenda can be discussed as an example of American idealism. "Economic independence" is based on the idea that government social programs give people things they have not earned, thus making them dependent on the government for handouts and taking

away their discipline, which is necessary to be economically independent and self-reliant. "Independence" is freedom from dependence on government programs. The idea behind strict
father economics is to force everybody to sink or swim, assuming anybody worth anything will swim—and we don't, and
shouldn't, care about those who sink. They lack discipline,
which shows they're not capable of acting morally, and so they
are not worthy and have no dignity.

Those who are newly independent, freed from dependence
on government programs like Social Security and Medicare, will
get new discipline and, with it, dignity and the security of being
able to fend for oneself. They will be able to pull themselves
up by their bootstraps and not have to "[labor] on the edge of
subsistence."

> In America's ideal of freedom, citizens find the dignity
> and security of economic independence, instead of labor-
> ing on the edge of subsistence. This is the broader defini-
> tion of liberty that motivated the Homestead Act, the
> Social Security Act, and the G.I. Bill of Rights.

This goes beyond merely political liberty. It is better than the
Homestead Act, the Social Security Act, and the G.I. Bill of
Rights. Those were government programs that gave you things—
land, a secure retirement, a college education—so that you could
use the common wealth to work for a better life. Bush reframes
the motivation behind those programs. Rather than uses of the
common wealth for the common good, they become opportunities to end dependence on government. Bush offers you freedom
from dependence on government, "a broader definition of liberty." The tens of millions of working Americans who cannot
even afford health care will now be made free—free to get their
own land, secure their own retirement, and pay for their own
college education and that of their children.

> And now we will extend this vision by reforming great in-
> stitutions to serve the needs of our time.

In radical conservative parlance, "reforming" means "destroying." Translation: We want to get rid of Social Security and
Medicare.

> To give every American a stake in the promise and future
> of our country, we will bring the highest standards to our
> schools,

But since funds for social programs like education are being
cut, there will be no funds to allow schools to meet those
standards.

> and build an ownership society. We will widen the owner-
> ship of homes and businesses, retirement savings and
> health insurance—preparing our people for the challenges
> of life in a free society. By making every citizen an agent
> of his or her own destiny, we will give our fellow Ameri-
> cans greater freedom from want and fear, and make our so-
> ciety more prosperous and just and equal.

The "challenges of life in a free society" means that you are free
of safety nets. Every citizen will become "an agent of his or her
own destiny." To meet those challenges as an agent of your own
destiny, you will have to become a successful entrepreneur and
businessperson. A great many people do not have those skills
and so will not be able to meet those challenges. They will be
impoverished, but that is just.

Radical conservatives believe that eliminating safety nets and
other government programs will actually give people the incentive to work harder, accomplish more, and become better entrepreneurs and investors. There is no concept of the cheap labor
trap here. No idea that many, many people have skills other than

entrepreneurial skill to bring to society. And there is an assumption that people are infinitely flexible and will—and should—all be entrepreneurs and savvy investors.

Next, the right's agenda for strict father morality—and its concept of character.

In America's ideal of freedom, the public interest depends on private character—on integrity, and tolerance toward others, and the rule of conscience in our own lives. Self-government relies, in the end, on the governing of the self.

That line again. The "governing of the self" is self-discipline, developed in strict father families through punishment when a child does wrong. You survive by internal discipline, called "character"—an "edifice" that is "upstanding" and "strong."

That edifice of character is built in families,

Strict father families . . .

supported by communities with standards,

that is, strict father moral standards you had better meet if you want community support,

and sustained in our national life by the truths of Sinai, the Sermon on the Mount, the words of the Koran, and the varied faiths of our people.

and morality in our national life exists only because of religion, because obedience to God guarantees our freedom.

Americans move forward in every generation by reaffirming all that is good and true that came before—ideals of justice and conduct that are the same yesterday, today, and forever.

Progress is possible only by following fixed moral truths— absolute right versus absolute wrong, now and forever.

Finally, there is the implicit agenda for conservative in-group compassion. "Freedom" from government programs and safety nets—"the challenge of living in a free society" and being "an agent of [one's] own destiny"—means that those who are weak, or aged, or disabled, or maimed, or injured will not have any right to basic sustenance and human dignity just because they are human beings. Instead, they will be thrown on the "mercy" of others—the kindness of strangers.

> In America's ideal of freedom, the exercise of rights is ennobled by service, and mercy, and a heart for the weak.

The ideal radical conservative shows his or her "nobility" by "service, mercy, and a heart for the weak." That's not much of a guarantee for the weak. Indeed, he is not addressing the weak.

> Liberty for all does not mean independence from one another. Our nation relies on men and women who look after a neighbor and surround the lost with love.

This is the ideal conservative community with occasional compassion for the worthy poor, where you "look after a neighbor," but not where the neighbor, by working all his or her life, has earned and deserves Social Security and Medicare.

> Americans, at our best, value the life we see in one another, and must always remember that even the unwanted have worth.

Outlaw abortion of unwanted children, but even though they "have worth," don't provide guaranteed pre- or postnatal care, or medical insurance, or food, or shelter, and don't protect them from environmental harms, or leave future generations a healthy economy free of debt. If you did, they wouldn't be "free" of government social programs.

Finally, there is the unity pitch:

> These questions that judge us also unite us, because Americans of every party and background, Americans by choice and by birth, are bound to one another in the cause of freedom.

We should come together and unite behind him, because we "are bound to one another in the cause of freedom."

> We have known divisions, which must be healed to move forward in great purposes—and I will strive in good faith to heal them. Yet those divisions do not define America. We felt the unity and fellowship of our nation when freedom came under attack, and our response came like a single hand over a single heart.

What brought us together on 9/11? Not empathy. Not care. Not a sense of identity with the people on those planes and in those towers. Not a sense of a common threat, or a common loss. No. "Like a single hand over a single heart." Like the Pledge of Allegiance—absolute blind loyalty to the nation-state. There must be loyalty to the moral authority, above all.

Finally, at the end, a return to democracy as religion.

> God moves and chooses as He wills. We have confidence because freedom is the permanent hope of mankind, the hunger in dark places, the longing of the soul. When our

Founders declared a new order of the ages; when soldiers died in wave upon wave for a union based on liberty; when citizens marched in peaceful outrage under the banner "Freedom Now"—they were acting on an ancient hope that is meant to be fulfilled. History has an ebb and flow of justice, but history also has a visible direction, set by liberty and the Author of Liberty.

God created liberty, the soul longs for it, history has a "visible direction"—God's plan, set by liberty and by God, who created liberty.

The use by the radical right of the language of "freedom" and "liberty" is no accident. It has been carefully crafted over many years and at great expense of money and resources. Right-wing think tanks like the Heritage Foundation, the American Enterprise Institute, and the Cato Institute use freedom and liberty as common themes, as do the most influential fundamentalist organizations like James Dobson's Focus on the Family and Jerry Falwell's Liberty Alliance, Liberty Home Bible Institute, and Liberty University.

Freedom and liberty are progressive ideas that are precious to Americans. When the right wing uses them, it sounds as if aliens had inhabited, and were trying to take possession of, the soul of America. It is time for an exorcism.

13

TAKING BACK FREEDOM

THINKING "FREEDOM" AND "LIBERTY"

Freedom and liberty are progressive ideas—our ideas. It is time for progressives to fully integrate them into our everyday thinking and into our language. Unless we keep pointing out over and over all the ways freedom and liberty are central to progressive thought, radical conservatives will wrest these most precious ideas from us and redefine them permanently. To take back freedom, we must remind ourselves regularly about the role of freedom in our lives.

Every progressive issue is ultimately about freedom, in the ways that we have discussed in Chapters 3 and 8. You give me a progressive issue, and I'll tell you how it comes down to a matter of freedom. Here are a few examples:

- Opportunity: The *freedom* to acquire the education, skills, and capital you need to realistically pursue fulfillment in life.
- Economic opportunity: The *freedom* to earn a living by working for a living. This requires *freedom* from the cheap labor trap.

- Health: Injury and illness impinge on *freedom*. Health keeps them from impinging on *freedom*.
- Social Security: Helps to guarantee *freedom* from want in old age.
- Unionization: The *freedom* of working people to organize so they can be *free* from want and fear through living wages, adequate benefits, and humane labor practices.
- Education: Provides the *freedom* needed for fulfillment in life, *freedom* from the barriers created by an insufficiency of knowledge and skill.
- Privacy: The *freedom* to pursue your personal life without disruption, interference, or the collection of personal knowledge about you by outsiders or by the state.

Freedom is an intimate part of your life as an American. Notice your freedoms. Work freedom into your everyday vocabulary. Use it or lose it.

AVOIDING PROGRESSIVE MISTAKES

Progressives make a lot of mistakes and conservatives just love to exploit them. Many of them are political mistakes—mistakes in political organizing, or failures in finding unity. Others are cognitive mistakes—mistakes in thinking and talking. Since I am a cognitive scientist, I will concentrate on the cognitive mistakes, mistakes in thought and language.

FRAMING MISTAKES

Mistakes in framing are extremely common among progressives. The most common mistake is to accept the right's frames. This traps you in their value system and their way of seeing the world. You wind up thinking in their terms instead of your own.

• *Stop using their words.*
Their mode of thought and their values come with their words. Just using "judicial activism," for example, accepts a frame in which (1) a judge is fair through being impersonal, mechanically applying the Constitution to cases at hand; (2) "activists" are emotional, irrational, and outside the mainstream; (3) liberal judges illegitimately impose their personal left-wing agendas from the bench and harm the country; (4) we must appoint conservative judges, who will stick to what is in the Constitution, not impose their own views, and that will be good for the country.

Every part of the frame is false. But if the public accepts the frame, the public will insist on radical conservative judges. Every time you use the words, you activate that frame in the brains of your listeners, thus helping to reinforce the frame and working against your own values.

What we need to do instead is to reframe from a progressive point of view. Talk instead about "freedom judges"—"judicial expansionists who have expanded our freedoms based on ideas there in the Constitution." We can then set up the frame of the expansion of freedoms that are implicit in the Constitution: the expansion of voting rights; of public education; of public health; of protections for consumers, workers, and the environment; of science; and so on. Radical conservative judges can then be described as they are: anti-freedom judges.

You can defuse the conservative frames of "strict construction" and "judicial activism" without mentioning them. Whenever a case reaches a high court, it is because it does not clearly fit within the established categories of the law. Judges have to either extend or narrow those categories, and when they do they change the law, in one way or another. The question is whether they change it in the direction of greater or lesser freedom. Are they expanding—or narrowing—voting rights, civil rights, fairness principles, public protections, privacy rights, education of the public, scientific knowledge, and other aspects of the public good? Do they want to take us back before the expansion of our freedoms or forward to a greater expansion of our freedoms? Are they profreedom or antifreedom?

The framing introduced is not just a matter of words or slogans. The expansion of freedom frame tells a deep truth. That truth defines a progressive mode of thought, what I call a fundamental frame. It is hardly original. The observation has been made many times. A variation on the theme—unity in the service of freedom—was used by Bill Clinton in his speech before the Democratic Convention in 2004:

> My friends, at every turning point in our history, we, the people, have chosen unity over division, heeding our founders' call to America's eternal mission to form a more perfect union, to widen the circle of opportunity deep in the reach of freedom and strengthen the bonds of our community. It happened every time, because we made the right choices.
>
> In the early days of the republic, America was divided and at a crossroads, much as it is today, deeply divided over whether or not to build a real nation with a national economy and a national legal system. We chose to build a more perfect union.
>
> In the Civil War, America was at another crossroads, deeply divided over whether to save the union and end slavery. We chose a more perfect union.

In the 1960s, when I was a young man, we were divided again over civil rights and women's rights. And again we chose to form a more perfect union.

What is new is the recognition that progressive freedom is the central idea in American life.

The expansion of freedom frame is general. It is not only about judicial activism; it applies to just about every issue. Take the 2005 bankruptcy bill, which had the effect of keeping poor people (though not wealthy corporations) from declaring bankruptcy in the face of overwhelming debt—in most cases debt from emergency medical care. This will keep tens of thousands of families enslaved to debt, often at the cost of their homes! It was sponsored and passed by conservatives. It was an antifreedom bill. It limited the economic freedom and the opportunity of poor and middle-class Americans. It was an assault on "ownership" and "opportunity"—conservative buzzwords that are Orwellian, used not with sincerity but rather to mean the very opposite.

Antifreedom bills are legion in the Congress as controlled by radical conservatives. The argument that they go against the grand tradition of progressive freedom in this country is a single argument that applies in case after case. The argument cannot be made only once. That will have no effect. It must be repeated over and over, on issue after issue. It is not a short-term strategy. It is a long-term strategy.

- *Avoid negating their frame.*

Negating their frame just activates the frame and traps you in a different way. Coming out against the president's tax relief plan—or even offering a plan for tax relief for the middle class—keeps the tax relief frame, with taxation as an affliction to be eliminated.

At the founding of this country, there was a clear understanding of the role of taxation in the government of a free society. States were called "commonwealths." The commonwealth idea was a simple freedom principle: In order for individuals to be maximally free to pursue their individual goals, you need to use the common wealth for the common good to build infrastructure needed by, and available to, everyone: roads, schools, and public buildings like courthouses, hospitals, jails, and arsenals. The role of a government is to do what individual citizens cannot: build the infrastructure needed for security and prosperity for all and provide access to freedom. That same freedom principle has been expanded throughout our history, as our freedoms have expanded. We used taxpayers' money to build the interstate highway system, the land grant colleges and public universities, the Internet, the federal regulatory system for banks and the stock market, and the court system, which is mostly used for corporate law. As we have discussed, no one can start a business, or prosper in big business, without such resources for individual freedom. Progressive taxation is fair because the wealthy use more of that infrastructure than the poor and so have more of a responsibility to maintain it. Again the issue isn't words or slogans, but the idea—a freedom principle called the common wealth.

The expansion of freedom frame and the common wealth frame express fundamental truths about our country, truths conceptualized via fundamental progressive frames—mental structures that are realized in our brains and characterize deep ideas that apply across the board to issue after issue. Once those ideas become part of our national consciousness, once they become implicit in public political discourse, they are there, ready to be used.

With the fundamental frames in place, it becomes much easier to craft powerful and lasting slogans that express surface frames—the progressive equivalents of the "death tax." You need deep fundamental frames to hook those surface frames to. The ultraright conservatives, over three decades, developed their system of fundamental frames and got them out into the public sphere. That's why their slogans expressing surface frames work.

Establishing fundamental frames in public discourse takes patience and perseverance. It is a necessary investment in the future. This is probably not going to be done by major political leaders, who tend to want slogans that will work effectively right away. These frames need to be established instead by progressives across the country—whoever is speaking out on issues, especially those in the media. It is a necessary part of taking back freedom.

THE RATIONALIST MISTAKE

A great many progressives function with a folk theory of the mind, based on a philosophical paradigm called rationalism. The folk version of rationalism is a myth about reason and its relationship to politics. It says that progressive thought came out of the Enlightenment in the form of rationalism.

The rationalist myth tells us that

- Reason is what defines our essence as human beings and sets us off from other animals.
- Therefore, reason is universal (all human beings have the same capacity for reason).
- Reason is conscious (we are aware of our thought).
- Reason is literal (it can directly fit the world).
- We all have an unconstrained free will.
- We are acting rationally when our free will follows the dictates of reason rather than our passions.
- It is irrational to be against your material self-interest. Therefore, reason serves to maximize our material self-interests.
- Because reason is universal, we can govern ourselves; we don't need the authority of the church or a king or aristocrats or experts.
- Since reason makes us equal as human beings, the best

form of government is a democracy—one that serves
the rational self-interests of all.

- Since facts matter for material interests, a rational government should promote access to the facts and should
support science.
- Universal reason gives rise to universal moral principles.

This idea comes in various philosophical versions, and their
corresponding folk versions, of what constitutes morality:

- Consequentialism: The rational consequences of your
actions for everyone, not just your actions themselves,
should be judged.
- Utilitarianism: The greatest good for the greatest number (a version of consequentialism).
- Kantianism: Treat everyone as an end in itself and
never as a means only.
- Rawlsianism: Act as if you had no knowledge of your
own place in society, as if you might have the lowliest
status.

The rationalist myth is social (about groups) and collectivist
(about everyone), rather than individualist (about individuals,
one at a time). It is antihierarchical (we share the *same* capacity
for reason, which makes us equal). It is literal—it does not admit
conceptual frames or conceptual metaphors—since reason has to
fit the world directly. Rationality is seen as conscious. Since reason is universal, the concepts used in reasoning are universally
shared. With the same concepts available to all, free will is not
constrained by the unavailability of concepts. All the above-
listed moral theories judge actions not in themselves but on the
basis of their effects on others.

Much of traditional liberalism was based on the rationalist
myth—as was traditional liberal economics, which assumed that

people acted like rational actors (maximizing self-interest), as well as liberal foreign policy, which assumed that nations also acted as rational actors (maximizing their national interests—their national wealth, military strength, and political influence).

Modern cognitive science has shown that this theory is false in just about every detail. Most thought is not conscious. Though some forms of reason are universal, much of reason is not, because we think using frames and conceptual metaphors, which need not be universal. Recent Nobel Prizes in Economics reflect this new, antirationalist knowledge about the mind: Rationality is bounded; thought uses frames, prototypes, and metaphors, which do not fit traditional rationality; and relevant knowledge is not shared. Economic decisions are largely made at an unconscious level. The neuroscientist Antonio Damasio has observed that reason is dependent on emotion, not independent of it; people with strokes and brain injuries that leave them unable to feel emotions or judge emotions in others cannot act rationally.

Many progressives still abide by aspects of the rationalist myth, which results in destructive political consequences for progressives. For example, rationalism claims that, since everybody is rational, you just need to tell people the facts and they will reason to the same right conclusion. That's just false, as we have learned from election after election. The facts alone will not set you free. If the frames that define common sense contradict the facts, the facts will be ignored. Cognitive science tells us why: The frames that define common sense are instantiated physically in the brain. When you hear a fact that is inconsistent with a physical structure in the brain (a frame), the physical structure (the frame) stays and the fact is ignored or explained away. Nonetheless, progressives keep using facts alone to argue against radical conservative frames.

What is needed is a new common sense that will naturally fit fundamental truths about the world and society.

If the rationalist myth were true, one could reason correctly as follows: Reason is conscious. Everyone can and should think rationally. Rational actors seek to maximize their self-interest. Therefore, pollsters and those who run focus groups should be able to ask voters what issues are most important for them and what policies would maximize their material self-interest, and voters should be able to tell them. Voters, being rational, should vote to maximize their material self-interest. Thus, if candidates take voters' six most important issues and craft programs to maximize voters' self-interest, voters, being rational, should vote for those candidates.

That's what the rationalist myth predicts, but it's not true. Voters may prefer the Democrats' positions on issues yet still vote Republican. Why?

THE WIRTHLIN EFFECT

Richard Wirthlin, Ronald Reagan's chief strategist for the 1980 and 1984 elections, writes in *The Greatest Communicator* about what he discovered when he went to work for Reagan in 1980. Wirthlin, a Berkeley-trained economist, had been educated in the rationalist tradition to think that voters voted on the basis of whether they agreed with a candidate's positions on the issues. Wirthlin discovered that voters tended not to agree with Reagan's positions on the issues, yet they liked Reagan. Wirthlin set out to find out why. His answer was that voters were voting on four closely linked criteria:

- Personal identification: They identified with Reagan.
- Values: Reagan spoke about values rather than programs and they liked his values.
- Trust: They trusted Reagan.
- Authenticity: They found Reagan authentic; he said what he believed and it showed.

So Wirthlin ran the campaigns on these criteria, and the rest is history—unfortunately for progressives and for the nation. The George W. Bush campaigns were run on the same principles.

It is not that positions on issues don't matter. They do. But they tend to be symbolic of values, identity, and character, rather than being of primary import in themselves. For example, if you identify yourself essentially as the mother or father in a strict father family, you may well be threatened by gay marriage, which is inconsistent with a strict father morality. For this reason, someone in the Midwest who has never even met anyone gay could have his or her deepest identity threatened by gay marriage. The issue is symbolic, not literal, and symbolism is powerful in politics.

THE PERSISTENCE OF RATIONALISM

Rationalism is alive and well among progressive candidates and their strategists—especially when it comes to "the center." In national elections, the voters tend to divide up as follows: strongly conservative Republican: 35–40 percent; strongly progressive Democrat: 35–40 percent; the center: 20–30 percent.

The rationalists see this as a continuum, defined by positions on issues alone. The rationalist idea is to take polls to find out what positions the voters prefer. A problem arises immediately. Conservatives have framed most issues using their language. Rationalists, who don't accept the existence of conceptual frames, see language as neutral and may take the conservative language as neutral. If presumably rationalist polls ask questions using conservative language, the issues will be framed from a conservative perspective, which will introduce a conservative bias into the polls. If the pollsters are not sensitive to framing, they may not notice such bias, and it will appear to them that the population is moving to the right. The rationalist prescription for a

Democratic candidate: If you want to attract more voters, move to the right.

It would be a tragic move. First, it helps the other side by activating their positions on the issues. Second, it alienates the progressive base, on which you depend. Third, it crosses the moral line between progressive and radical conservative worldviews. By asserting conservative moral positions, you are not sticking to your values.

Conservatives know better. They don't try to get more votes by moving to the left. Why? They understand that the people in the center are biconceptuals, with strict morality governing certain aspects of their lives and nurturant morality governing other aspects. Which governs politics—strict or nurturant morality—can shift. It depends on which version of morality is activated for politics in this election. To activate your version of morality, you use the language of your moral system. That is, you talk to the center using the same language as you use with your base.

Except in two classes of cases. On the national level, conservatives know that, on the issues, they are a minority. They have to activate the strict father model in a majority of biconceptuals. They also have to be sure they don't turn them off. For example, many biconceptuals are conservative in economic, social, and religious domains, but progressive in the environmental domain. Simply put, they love the land. Hiking and camping with the family, hunting and fishing with friends, perhaps they even want to save God's creation. So when the Bush administration wants to gut the Clean Air Act and replace it with a bill that allows dirtier air, it knows that it cannot use the name the Dirty Air Act. The result is that they use Orwellian language: the Clear Skies Initiative. No one, not even a staunch conservative, is against "Clear Skies," though if you know the bill, you know "Clear Skies" means dirtier air. This is lying with language. But it is not moving to the left on policy.

Besides Orwellian language, conservatives also speak to biconceptuals using uncontested versions of contested concepts, as we saw in the case of freedom. In short, they use words like "opportunity," "security," and "fairness" in contexts that fit their uncontested senses. The effect is to be compatible with whatever meaning those in the audience have, no matter what their politics.

THE BIGGEST RATIONALIST MISTAKE

Because rationalists see reason as conscious and literal, they miss framing and worldview effects. If you don't believe that there are different, metaphorically defined worldviews, and if you don't believe there are deep fundamental frames that determine how people reason across issue areas, then what are you to make of the enterprise of reframing? You are going to see it as a form of spin or propaganda, of using words to fool people. This is the worst rationalist mistake of all, because it hides the entire conceptual dimension of politics—all the frames, metaphors, prototypes, and narratives that give political thought and language its moral and emotional depth, complexity, and color.

In short, there are five major rationalist mistakes:

- Believing that you can argue effectively against established frames with raw facts—that is, thinking that the truth will set you free
- Believing that voters vote on candidates' positions on the issues, rather than on identity, values, trust, and authenticity—and on the symbolic value of the issues
- Believing that candidates should follow the polls, rather than try to change them
- Ignoring how biconceptuals work
- Believing that reframing is just spin or propaganda, rather than a means of telling deep truths effectively

Does the failure of the rationalist myth mean that we should give up on reason and truth? Not at all. Instead, we should pay attention to cognitive science and get reason right so people can better see the truth about our social, political, and economic realities. What we need is a "higher rationality."

FREEDOM ISN'T FREE

Freedom isn't free. It isn't something that was won for us back in 1776. We can't take it for granted or just pass it on effortlessly to our children. The progressive freedoms that have defined our country have been expanded over time with great effort and sacrifice, and they are being beaten back and taken from us. Not by foreign enemies. Not by terrorists. But by radical conservatives, who are fellow Americans. It would be easy to say that they are hypocrites, not meaning what they say. Sometimes they are; many of them do lie and use Orwellian language. But on the whole, they do say what they mean. It would be easy to say that the radical conservatives are all evil, or greedy, or cruel, or irrational, or just plain stupid. But they are no more like that than the rest of us. It would be easy to say they are immoral. But they function with a morality of their own—one that we find immoral. It would be easy to say that they are not loyal Americans, not patriotic, not freedom loving. But they consider themselves even more patriotic than we are, and sincerely use "freedom" and "liberty" as their watchwords. It would be easy if we controlled the language of "freedom" and "liberty"—the language of our deepest values. But we don't. They have commandeered our words and changed their meaning. We must take back the words, restore their meaning, and then do the hard work of taking back our government.

There are two kinds of work that must be done. The first is

political—uniting, organizing, recruiting candidates, training candidates and campaign workers, canvassing, building coalitions, and working though the media. Political work is relatively well understood and just takes money, organization, dedication, and hard work. Winning elections is crucial. But winning more elections—even taking back the House, the Senate, and the presidency, however necessary—is not enough. We must take back the very idea that defines our country—freedom. Unless that is done, the culture wars will continue, they will keep our country divided and make it less likely that elections alone will serve the cause of real freedom.

Beyond the political work is the cognitive work—working on your own mind. This requires changing your brain, thinking in ways you have never thought before, understanding what you have not previously understood, and talking and listening in new ways. The cognitive work is more difficult than the day-to-day political work—partly because the political work is more familiar, and partly because cognitive work just is difficult.

A HIGHER RATIONALITY

What makes the cognitive work so hard is that it requires a new, higher rationality. We are used to thinking without thinking about it. We now have to become aware of how we and others are thinking and talking. We grew up assuming common sense. We now have to understand that one person's common sense is another's oppressive political ideology. We grew up thinking that freedom is freedom is freedom, that the word names a single common idea. We now have to be aware of contested concepts, that "freedom" means something radically different to the radical right—and so do other important words like "opportunity," "fairness," "responsibility," "harm," "compassion," and even "God."

"SHOCKER!"

On January 24, 2006, *The New York Times' Science Times* section ran a story with the headline "A Shocker: Partisan Thought Is Unconscious." It was a report of a study by a team led by Drew Westen of Emory University.

> Using M.R.I. scanners, neuroscientists have now tracked what happens in the politically partisan brain when it tries to digest damning facts about favored candidates or criticisms of them. The process is almost entirely emotional and unconscious, the researchers report, and there are flares of activity in the brain's pleasure centers when unwelcome information is being rejected.
>
> In 2004, the researchers recruited 30 adult men who described themselves as committed Republicans or Democrats. The men, half of them supporters of President Bush and the other half backers of Senator John Kerry, earned $50 to sit in an M.R.I. machine and consider several statements in quick succession.
>
> The first was a quote attributed to one of the two candidates: either a remark by Mr. Bush in support of Kenneth L. Lay, the former Enron chief, before he was indicted, or a statement by Mr. Kerry that Social Security should be overhauled. Moments later, the participants read a remark that showed the candidate reversing his position. The quotes were doctored for maximum effect but presented as factual.
>
> The Republicans in the study judged Mr. Kerry as harshly as the Democrats judged Mr. Bush. But each group let its own candidate off the hook.
>
> After the participants read the contradictory comment, the researchers measured increased activity in several areas of the brain. They included a region involved in

regulating negative emotions and another called the cingulate, which activates when the brain makes judgments about forgiveness, among other things. Also, a spike appeared in several areas known to be active when people feel relieved or rewarded. The "cold reasoning" regions of the cortex were relatively quiet.

To cognitive scientists this is hardly a "shocker." Results of this sort have been known for more than thirty years, though it is wonderful to have MRI confirmation of what we would expect from three decades of research. The Westen team is to be congratulated. We knew that deep-seated frames would trump the facts. The role of cingulate and other brain regions was not known in advance, but it is not a surprise.

What is sad is that the *Science Times* found it "A Shocker" that "Partisan Thought Is Unconscious," when results about the unconscious nature of thought have been commonplace for three decades. The question is, How long will it take for the news and editorial departments of the *Times* to catch up to the science section?

The problem, of course, lies less with the *Times* and other media than with the universities that train the journalists, pundits, candidates, staffs, pollsters, and strategists. Students of the social sciences and of communications rarely learn about even the most elementary properties of mind and brain. Public political discourse—in government, in the media, in the think tanks, and in the universities—has not incorporated even the most basic facts.

Perhaps the hardest reframing problem is reframing our own minds.

FREEING FREE WILL

What makes cognitive work so urgent and vital is that it affects free will itself. You can't will something if you have no idea what it is. Before free will can operate, you must be able to conceptualize what you are willing. Since you can't conceptualize without concepts, you can't take back progressive freedom unless you know what progressive freedom is, that we are losing it, and what is replacing it.

This book is about more than freedom in the political and patriotic sense. It is just as much about free will, about how we have begun to lose it and how to regain it. Parallel to the right-wing political machine is a right-wing mind machine. It works via language in at least two ways. First, via words and idioms, like "death tax," "tax relief," "judicial activism," "war against terror," "liberal elites," "defending freedom," "pro-life," "tax and spend," "legislate from the bench," "cut spending," "up-or-down vote," "homosexual lifestyle," "ownership society," "cut and run," and so on. Second, via arguments, such as "It's your money. You earned it. You can spend it better than the government can."

The language evokes ideas—in the form of frames and conceptual metaphors—and complex frame sequences in the case of arguments. As the language is repeated, the frames and metaphors become activated in the brain over and over, and finally become physically fixed in the brain through changes at the synapses. As your brain and its concepts are changed, free will is changed because you can will only what you can conceptualize. If taxes are only afflictions to be removed, if education is only teaching to the test, if poverty is deserved for lack of discipline, if stem-cell research is child mutilation, if homosexuality is only a lifestyle, if religious freedom is government-supported proselytizing, if scientific theories are merely beliefs—if this is the only way you think about these matters, then your free will is severely limited because you cannot even imagine how most

Americans understand these issues, much less act on that understanding. The conservative mind-and-message machine can radically change—and disastrously limit—one's free will, and it has
been working away for more than thirty years.

Real freedom requires a higher rationality—a mode of
thought in which one can recognize ideological framing, in
which one can see the ideology behind the language and tell
whether a phrase or an argument is based on a strict or nurturant
value system. It is a mode of thought in which one can see who's
using "freedom" with what meaning, and what is meant in context by other contested concepts like opportunity and responsibility.

PUBLIC DISCOURSE AND THE MEDIA

To serve freedom, public discourse requires a higher rationality as
well. And some professions have an enormous responsibility for
keeping public discourse free and open.

Journalists are crucial guardians of our freedom in this respect, and they are doing very badly when it comes to higher rationality. The political interview show hosts use conservative
language as if it were neutral. Print journalists typically accept
the radical conservative framing of issues—both the ideas and
the language.

A quick check of Google News at this writing turned up
3,060 news stories using "tax relief" as if it were a neutral term,
as well as 3,760 for "cut and run," 1,060 for "cut spending," and
537 for "judicial activism."

The journalistic commentary right after President Bush's second inaugural address showed little or no understanding that he
was using "freedom" in a radical conservative sense, a sense foreign to the American tradition.

Only a right-wing think tank, the Claremont Institute, did report correctly that the speech called for the reversal of the notion of freedom introduced by President Roosevelt—freedom from want and fear. Ken Masugi writes on their Web site:

> Is this an extension of FDR's "second bill of rights," one assuring security, which he proposed because the Founders' political rights "proved inadequate to assure us equality in the pursuit of happiness"? FDR asserts, "We have come to the clear realization of the fact that true individual freedom cannot exist without economic security and independence. 'Necessitous men are not free men.'" Sixty years ago FDR concluded, in his January 11, 1944, address to Congress, "unless there is security here at home there cannot be lasting peace in the world."
>
> Bush's speech should be read as a reply to FDR and an attempted reversal of the process he started domestically, while affirming its international presence but bypassing the United Nations FDR supported. Bush would maintain America as a force in the world and use that commitment to bring more freedom to America.
>
> Bush appears to be aiming at a grand political realignment here, one that questions the very basis of the Progressivism that undermined American constitutionalism.

It should not be surprising that it was an overtly radical conservative think tank, not the media, that interpreted the speech correctly as a radical reversal of previously hailed American freedoms. A quick Google check could have uncovered this, but no journalists did the check.

Moreover, even if journalists had found this analysis, they would most likely not have reported it because they had not prepared the public for the president's hidden agenda, telegraphed in a kind of code to the right-wing base, while appearing superficially to say the opposite. Bush had said that "by making every citizen an agent of his or her own destiny, we will give our fellow Americans greater freedom from want and fear and make our society more prosperous and just and equal." But rather than endorsing FDR's "freedom from want and fear" via Social Security, support of unions, and social programs, Bush would "[make] every citizen an agent of his or her own destiny." That is, he would replace public responsibility with private responsibility: privatize Social Security, eliminate unions, and destroy social programs, leaving everyone—strong or weak, young or old—to fend for himself or herself, for better or more often for worse.

Balance of sound bites is no cure because there is no background given that enlightens the reader or viewer either about issues of truth, or about how the words are being used. Here is an all-too-typical example from the *San Francisco Chronicle* (December 12, 2005). The story is about a lawsuit by the Association of Christian Schools International against the University of California for religious bias in refusing to accept certain courses at Calvary Chapel Christian School as meeting freshman admission requirements.

> The lawsuit marks a new front in America's culture wars, in which the largest organization of Christian schools in the country and the University of California, which admitted 50,017 freshmen this year, are accusing each other of trying to abridge or constrain each others' freedom.

The reporter is right that freedom is at the center of the case. Here are the sound bites on freedom that he includes. First, the Christian schools:

> The rejections, the suit asserted, "violate the freedom of speech of Christian schools, students and teachers." . . . Wendell Bird, lead attorney for the schools, believes,

"This is a liberty case, the right of nonpublic institutions to be free . . . It's very troubling to the largest Christian school organization in the country because it restrains freedom and could spread."

It is never explained why UC's refusal to accept a small number of courses for admission requirements is an abridgment of the schools' freedom of speech, or freedom in general.

UC's response is twofold: First, the UC attorney Christopher Patti takes the charge of abridgment of freedom of speech at face value and goes on the defense: "The university is not telling these schools what they can and can't teach." Second, a UC counsel responds with a counter charge: "This lawsuit is really an attempt to control the regents' educational choices. Plaintiffs seek to constrain the regents' exercise of its First Amendment–protected right of academic freedom to establish admissions criteria."

What is left out are the conflicting views of what constitutes freedom, though there is a hint. One of the rejected texts, *Biology for Christian Schools*, states, "the people who have prepared this book have tried consistently to put the Word of God first and science second. [If] at any point God's Word is not put first, the author apologizes."

Fundamentalists interpret the freedom to practice their religion as guaranteed by the government to mean (1) the freedom to take their interpretation of the Bible as literal truth, (2) the freedom to teach that "truth," (3) government support for that freedom, that is, for the teaching of their "truth" in public institutions and institutions that receive public funds, and (4) the freedom to teach their beliefs as if they have a right be aired on an equal footing with real science and real scholarship. Anything less is not seen as governmental protection of the freedom of religion and freedom of speech. This view of religious liberty, which lies behind this lawsuit, is almost never spelled out in the media.

Academic freedom, on the other hand, recognizes academic institutions as special places dedicated to truth and knowledge as determined by academic and scientific standards—free from religious dogma, political expediency, or other external interference. This is related to political progressivism by the progressive commitment to open inquiry and to the responsibility to fit external reality as well as possible via the use of evidence and reason.

Though the author mentions that the suit is part of the culture wars, it is never explained what the culture wars are centrally about and exactly why and how freedom has become the central values issue in this suit.

This is the kind of understanding required by a higher rationality. It is a high standard for journalism and the media to meet. But ultimately, informed public discourse will require such a standard. Now is the time to start. There is a lot of cognitive work to do, not just among ordinary citizens, but also among the journalists, political leaders, educators, and clergy who shape public discourse.

THE CHALLENGE

Higher rationality is hard to achieve. It is hard to go beyond the Punch-and-Judy journalism where people with different worldviews scream past each other. It is hard to go beyond the Punch-and-Judy show of everyday life, at the office, at the holiday dinner table, with neighbors, hard not to feel anything more than frustration and anger at people you find immoral, irrational, and uninformed—and proud of it, proud of their patriotism and their common sense. It is hard to recognize that what passes for common sense can be terribly mistaken.

We were raised to think that words are transparent, that they have single simple meanings that directly fit reality. We were not raised to think in terms of contested concepts that have uncontested cores and virtually opposite extended meanings. We were not raised to think in terms of frames and metaphorical ideas. And we were not raised to think in terms of alternative world-views—that our countrymen and even our next-door neighbors might see the world in a radically different way. In short, we were not raised to see certain deep truths that are essential to our freedom. Transcending the ideas that we were raised with—growing to see more—is the cognitive work of achieving freedom.

SUGGESTED READING

These references allow the reader to enter the literature; they are not exhaustive. They are divided into the following areas: Web sites, contemporary politics, cognitive science and cognitive linguistics, and freedom/philosophy.

WEB SITES

MAJOR WEB CITATIONS

George W. Bush's Second Inaugural Address can be found at www.whitehouse
.gov/inaugural.

Bill Clinton's address to the 2004 Democratic National Convention can be
found at www.cbsnews.com/stories/2004/07/26/politics/main632008.shtml.

PROGRESSIVE WEB SITES USED

Alternet, an online magazine and blog: www.alternet.org

Daily Kos, the blog of blogs: www.dailykos.com

Huffington Post, an online magazine and blog: www.huffingtonpost.com

Media Matters, David Brock's Web site: www.mediamatters.org

Sirota Blog: www.davidsirota.com

Rockridge Institute: www.rockridgeinstitute.org (The main site for postings relevant to the topics of this book)

CONSERVATIVE WEB SITES USED

Acton Institute for the Study of Religion and Liberty: www.acton.org

American Enterprise Institute: www.aei.org

Catholic Community Forum: www.catholic-forum.com

Cato Institute: www.cato.org

Claremont Institute: www.claremont.org

Dial-a-Truth Ministries: www.av1611.org/wwjd.html
Focus on the Family: www.family.org
The Free Market, the Mises Institute monthly: www.mises.org/freemarket_detail
 .asp?control=432&sortorder=articledate>
Global Catholic Network: www.ewtn.com
Heritage Foundation: www.heritage.org
Ludwig von Mises Institute: www.mises.org
National Review Online: www.nationalreview.com

BOOKS AND OTHER SOURCES

This book is about ideas. There are many excellent books on the facts relevant
to these ideas. Some first-rate places to start are John Schwarz's *Freedom Reclaimed*, Thomas Frank's *What's the Matter with Kansas?*, Jacob Hacker and Paul
Pierson's *Off Center*, and David Sirota's *Hostile Takeover*.

BOOKS BY THE AUTHOR
Moral Politics provides a much more detailed view of the strict father and nurturant parent models than was possible here.
Don't Think of an Elephant! is the easiest place to start reading about framing.
Metaphors We Live By (with Mark Johnson) offers an easy and enjoyable introduction to the theory of metaphorical thought, as does Zoltán Kövecses's
 introductory text *Metaphor*.
Philosophy in the Flesh (with Mark Johnson) is a useful reference for the theory
 of conceptual metaphor, for philosophical issues in general, and for philosophical topics like causation, essence, teleology, and morality.
Women, Fire, and Dangerous Things is an introduction to basic findings about
 concepts in cognitive science. It also contains a detailed survey of basic results on categorization and multiple word meanings.
More Than Cool Reason (with Mark Turner) is a survey of types of poetic
 metaphors that shows how poetic uses of metaphor depend on everyday
 metaphorical thought.
Where Mathematics Comes From (with Rafael Núñez) demonstrates that higher
 mathematics is both embodied and makes essential and very extensive use
 of metaphorical thought.
My paper with Vittorio Gallese, "The Brain's Concepts," shows, on the basis of
 mirror neuron research, what a possible neural mechanism might be for the
 instantiation of frames in the physical brain.

CONTEMPORARY POLITICS
Armstrong, Jerome, and Markos Moulitsas Zúniga. *Crashing the Gates: Netroots,
 Grassroots, and the Rise of the People-Powered Politics*. White River Junction,
 VT: Chelsea Green, 2006.

Bartkowski, John P. *The Promise Keepers: Servants, Soldiers, and Godly Men.* Brunswick, NJ: Rutgers University Press, 2004.

———. *Remaking the Godly Marriage: Gender Negotiation in Evangelical Families.* New Brunswick, NJ: Rutgers University Press, 2001.

Carter, Jimmy. *Our Endangered Values: America's Moral Crisis.* New York: Simon and Schuster, 2005.

Court, Jamie. *Corporateering: How Corporate Power Steals Your Personal Freedom—and What You Can Do About It.* New York: Jeremy Tarcher, 2003.

Domke, David. *God Willing? Political Fundamentalism in the White House, the "War on Terror" and the Echoing Press.* Ann Arbor, MI: Pluto Press, 2004.

Feldman, Noah. *Divided by God: America's Church-State Problem—and What We Should Do About It.* New York: Farrar, Straus and Giroux, 2005.

Frank, Thomas. *What's the Matter with Kansas? How Conservatives Won the Heart of America.* New York: Metropolitan Books, 2004.

Hacker, Jacob S., and Paul Pierson. *Off Center: The Republican Revolution and the Erosion of American Democracy.* New Haven: Yale University Press, 2005.

Hannity, Sean. *Let Freedom Ring: Winning the War of Liberty over Liberalism.* New York: HarperCollins, 2002.

Lerner, Michael. *The Left Hand of God: Taking Back Our Country from the Religious Right.* San Francisco: HarperSanFrancisco, 2005.

Loehr, Davidson. *America, Fascism, and God: Sermons from a Heretical Preacher.* White River Junction, VT: Chelsea Green, 2005.

Micklethwait, John, and Adrian Wooldridge. *The Right Nation: Conservative Power in America.* New York: Penguin, 2004.

Mooney, Chris. *The Republican War on Science.* New York: Basic Books, 2005.

Packer, George. *The Assassins' Gate: America in Iraq.* New York: Farrar, Straus and Giroux, 2005.

Santorum, Rick. *It Takes a Family: Conservatism and the Common Good.* Wilmington, DE: ISI Books, 2005.

Schwarz, John E. *Freedom Reclaimed: Rediscovering the American Vision.* Baltimore: Johns Hopkins University Press, 2005.

Sirota, David. *Hostile Takeover: How Big Business Bought Our Government and How We Can Take It Back.* New York: Crown, 2006.

Wallis, Jim. *God's Politics: Why the Right Gets It Wrong and the Left Doesn't Get It.* San Francisco: HarperSanFrancisco, 2005.

Wirthlin, Dick, with Wynton C. Hall. *The Great Communicator: What Ronald Reagan Taught Me About Politics, Leadership and Life.* Hoboken, NJ: John Wiley, 2004.

COGNITIVE SCIENCE AND COGNITIVE LINGUISTICS

Boroditsky, Lera. "Evidence for Metaphoric Representations: Perspective in Space and Time." In *Proceedings of the Nineteenth Annual Conference of the Cognitive Science Society,* edited by Pat Langley and Michael G. Shafto. Mahwah, NJ: Lawrence Erlbaum, 1997.

Churchland, Patricia Smith. *Neurophilosophy: Toward a Unified Science of the Mind/Brain*. Cambridge, MA: MIT Press, 1986.

———, and Terrence J. Sejnowski. *The Computational Brain*. Cambridge, MA: MIT Press, 1992.

Churchland, Paul. *The Engine of Reason, the Seat of the Soul: A Philosophical Journey into the Brain*. Cambridge, MA: MIT Press, 1995.

Crick, Francis. *The Astonishing Hypothesis: The Scientific Search for the Soul*. New York: Scribner, 1994.

Damasio, Antonio R. *Descartes' Error: Emotion, Reason, and the Human Brain*. New York: Putnam, 1994.

Dehaene, Stanislas. *The Number Sense: How the Mind Creates Mathematics*. New York: Oxford University Press, 1997.

De Valois, Russell L., and Karen K. De Valois. "Neural Coding of Color." In *Handbook of Perception*. Vol. V, *Seeing*, edited by Edward C. Careterette and Morton P. Friedman. New York: Academic Press, 1975.

Edelman, Gerald M. *Bright Air, Brilliant Fire: On the Matter of Mind*. New York: Basic Books, 1992.

Fauconnier, Gilles. *Mappings in Thought and Language*. New York: Cambridge University Press, 1997.

———. *Mental Spaces: Aspects of Meaning Construction in Natural Language*. Cambridge, MA: MIT Press, 1985.

Feldman, J., and S. Narayanan. "Embodied Meaning in a Neural Theory of Language." *Brain and Language* 89 (2004): 385–92.

Feldman, Jerome A. *From Molecule to Metaphor: A Neural Theory of Language*. Cambridge, MA: MIT Press, 2006.

Fillmore, Charles J. "Semantics." In *Linguistics in the Morning Calm*, edited by the Linguistic Society of Korea, 111–38. Seoul: Hanshin, 1982.

———. "Frames and the Semantics of Understanding." *Quaderni di Semantica* 6 (1985): 222–53.

———. *Lectures on Deixis*. Stanford, CA: CSLI Publications, 1992.

Gallese, Vittorio. "Being Like Me: Self-Other Identity, Mirror Neurons and Empathy." In *Perspectives on Imitation: From Cognitive Neuroscience to Social Science*, edited by Susan Hurley and Nick Chater. Cambridge, MA: MIT Press, 2004.

———. "Embodied Simulation: From Neurons to Phenomenal Experience." *Phenomenology and the Cognitive Sciences* 4 (2005): 23–48.

———, and George Lakoff. "The Brain's Concepts: The Role of the Sensory-Motor System in Reason and Language." *Cognitive Neuropsychology* 23, nos. 3–4 (May–June 2005): 455–79.

Gallie, W. B. "Essentially Contested Concepts." *Proceedings of the Aristotelian Society* 167 (1956).

Gibbs, Raymond W., Jr. *The Poetics of Mind: Figurative Thought, Language, and Understanding*. New York: Cambridge University Press, 1994.

Goffman, Erving. *Frame Analysis: Essays on the Organization of Experience*. New York: Harper, 1974.

Grady, Joseph. "Foundations of Meaning: Primary Metaphors and Primary Scenes." PhD diss., University of California at Berkeley, 1997.

Holland, Dorothy, and Naomi Quinn, eds. *Cultural Models in Language and Thought*. New York: Cambridge University Pres, 1987.

Hubel, David H. *Eye, Brain, and Vision*. New York: Scientific American Library, 1988.

Jeannerod, Marc. *The Cognitive Neuroscience of Action*. Cambridge, MA: Blackwell, 1997.

Johnson, Christopher R. "Constructional Grounding: The Role of Interpretational Overlap in Lexical and Constructional Acquisition." PhD diss., University of California at Berkeley, 1999.

Johnson, Mark. *The Body in the Mind: The Bodily Basis of Meaning, Imagination, and Reason*. Chicago: University of Chicago Press, 1987.

———. *Moral Imagination: Implications of Cognitive Science for Ethics*. Chicago: University of Chicago Press, 1993.

———, ed. *Philosophical Perspectives on Metaphor*. Minneapolis: University of Minnesota Press, 1981.

Kahneman, Daniel, ed. "A Perspective on Judgment and Choice: Mapping Bounded Rationality." *American Psychologist* 58, no. 9 (September 2003): 697–720.

———. "A Psychological Perspective on Economics." *American Economic Review* 93, no. 2 (May 1, 2003): 162–68.

———, and Amos Tversky, eds. *Choices, Values and Frames*. New York: Russell Sage Foundation, 2000.

Kay, Paul, and Chad K. McDaniel. "The Linguistic Significance of the Meanings of Basic Color Terms." *Language* 54 (1978): 610–46.

Kövecses, Zoltán. *Emotion Concepts*. New York: Springer-Verlag, 1990.

———. *Metaphor: A Practical Introduction*. New York: Oxford University Press, 2002.

———. *Metaphor in Culture: Universality and Variation*. New York: Cambridge University Press, 2005.

Lakoff, George. "The Contemporary Theory of Metaphor." In *Metaphor and Thought*, 2d ed., edited by Andrew Ortony, 202–51. New York: Cambridge University Press, 1993.

———. *Don't Think of an Elephant! Know Your Values and Frame the Debate*. White River Junction, VT: Chelsea Green, 2004.

———. *Moral Politics: What Conservatives Know That Liberals Don't*. 2d ed. Chicago: University of Chicago Press, 2002.

———. *Women, Fire, and Dangerous Things: What Categories Reveal About the Mind*. Chicago: University of Chicago Press, 1987.

Lakoff, George, and Mark Johnson. *Metaphors We Live By*. 2d ed. Chicago: University of Chicago Press, 2003.

———. *Philosophy in the Flesh: The Embodied Mind and Its Challenge to Western Thought*. New York: Basic Books, 1999.

Lakoff, George, and Rafael E. Núñez. *Where Mathematics Comes From: How the Embodied Mind Brings Mathematics into Being*. New York: Basic Books, 2000.

Lakoff, George, and Mark Turner. *More Than Cool Reason: A Field Guide to Poetic Metaphor*. Chicago: University of Chicago Press, 1989.

Mervis, Carolyn B., and Eleanor Rosch. "Categorization of Natural Objects." *Annual Review of Psychology* 32 (1981): 89–115.

Narayanan, Srinivas. "Talking the Talk Is Like Walking the Walk: A Computational Model of Verbal Aspect." *Proceedings of the Nineteenth Annual Conference of the Cognitive Science Society* (1997).

Regier, Terry. *The Human Semantic Potential: Spatial Language and Constrained Connectionism*. Cambridge, MA: MIT Press, 1996.

Rizzolatti, Giacomo, and Laila Craighero. "The Mirror Neuron System." *Annual Review of Neuroscience* 27 (July 2004): 169–92.

Rosch, E. "Human Categorization." In *Studies in Cross-Cultural Psychology*, edited by Neil Warren. New York: Academic Press, 1977.

———. "Principles of Categorization." In *Cognition and Categorization*, edited by E. Rosch and B. B. Lloyd, 27–48. Hillsdale, NJ: Lawrence Erlbaum, 1978.

———, C. B. Mervis, W. Gray, D. Johnson, and P. Boyes-Braem. "Basic Objects in Natural Categories." *Cognitive Psychology* 8 (1976): 382–439.

Schank, Roger C., and Robert P. Abelson. *Scripts, Plans, Goals, and Understanding: An Inquiry into Human Knowledge Structures*. Hillsdale, NJ: Lawrence Erlbaum, 1977.

Sweetser, Eve. *From Etymology to Pragmatics: Metaphorical and Cultural Aspects of Semantic Structure*. New York: Cambridge University Press, 1990.

Taylor, John R. *Linguistic Categorization: Prototypes in Linguistic Theory*. New York: Oxford University Press, 1989.

Tversky, Amos, and Daniel Kahneman. "Rational Choice and the Framing of Decisions." In *Decision Making: Descriptive, Normative, and Prescriptive Interactions*, edited by David E. Bell, Howard Raiff, and Amos Tversky, 167–92. New York: Cambridge University Press, 1988.

Winter, Steven L. *A Clearing in the Forest: Law, Life, and Mind*. Chicago: University of Chicago Press, 2001.

Zeki, Semir. *A Vision of the Brain*. Boston: Blackwell, 1993.

FREEDOM / PHILOSOPHY

Aristotle. *Nicomachean Ethics*. Trans. W. D. Ross. In *The Basic Works of Aristotle*, edited by Richard McKeon. New York: Random House. 1941.

Austin, J.L. *How to Do Things with Words*. Cambridge, MA: Harvard University Press, 1975.

Berlin, Isaiah. *Liberty*. New York: Oxford University Press, 2002.

Connolly, William E. *The Terms of Political Discourse*. 3d ed. Princeton: Princeton University Press, 1993.

Day, J. P. *Liberty and Justice*. Wolfeboro, NH: Croom Helm, 1987.

Descartes, René. *Discourse on Method*. In *The Philosophical Works of Descartes*, edited and translated by Elizabeth S. Haldane and G.R.T. Ross. Cambridge: Cambridge University Press, 1970.

Dworkin, Ronald. *Taking Rights Seriously*. Cambridge, MA: Harvard University Press, 1977.

Flathman, Richard E. *The Philosophy of Politics and Freedom*. Chicago: University of Chicago Press, 1987.

Foner, Eric. *Give Me Liberty! An American History*. New York: Norton, 2004.

———. *The Story of American Freedom*. New York: Norton, 1998.

Friedman, Milton. *Capitalism and Freedom*. 40th anniversary ed. Chicago: University of Chicago Press, 1982.

Gray, John. *Hayek on Liberty*. New York: Routledge, 1998.

———. *Liberalisms: Essays in Political Philosophy*. New York: Routledge, 1989.

Gray, Tim. *Freedom*. Atlantic Highlands, NJ: Humanities Press, 1991.

Hart, H.L.A., and Tony Honoré. *Causation in the Law*. Cambridge, MA: Harvard University Press, 1958.

Hayek, Friedrich A. *The Constitution of Liberty*. Chicago: University of Chicago Press, 1960.

———. *The Road to Serfdom*. 50th anniversary ed. Chicago: University of Chicago Press, 1994.

Kant, Immanuel. *Grounding for the Metaphysics of Morals* and *Metaphysics of Morals*. Trans. James W. Ellington. In *[Kant's] Ethical Philosophy*. Indianapolis: Hackett, 1983.

———. *Lectures on Ethics*. Trans. Louis Infield. Indianapolis: Hackett, 1980.

Kirk, Russell. *The Conservative Mind: From Burke to Eliot*. Washington, DC: Regnery, 1986.

Kristjánsson, Kristján. *Social Freedom: The Responsibility View*. New York: Cambridge University Press, 1990.

Kymlicka, Will. *Contemporary Political Philosophy*. New York: Oxford University Press, 1990.

Locke, John. *Two Treatises of Government*. Cambridge: Cambridge University Press, 1960.

Lukes, Steven. *Moral Conflict and Politics*. Oxford: Clarendon Press, 1991.

MacIntyre, Alasdair. *After Virtue: A Study in Moral Theory*. 2d ed. Notre Dame, IN: University of Notre Dame Press, 1984.

Mill, John Stuart. *On Liberty*. New York: Prometheus, 1986.

Miller, D. *Liberty*. New York: Oxford University Press, 1991.

Nash, George H. *The Conservative Intellectual Movement in America Since 1945*. New York: Basic Books, 1976.

Nozick, Robert. *Anarchy, State and Utopia*. New York: Basic Books, 1974.

Plato. *Republic*. Trans Paul Shorey. In *The Collected Dialogues of Plato*, edited by Edith Hamilton and Huntington Cairns. Princeton: Princeton University Press, 1961.

Rawls, John A. *A Theory of Justice*. Cambridge, MA: Harvard University Press, 1971.

Sen, Amartya. *Development as Freedom*. New York: Knopf, 1999.

———. *Rationality and Freedom*. Cambridge, MA: Harvard University Press, 2002.

Spencer, Herbert. *The Man Versus the State*. Indianapolis: Liberty Classics, 1981.

Swanton, Christine. *Freedom: A Coherence Theory*. Indianapolis: Hackett, 1992.

ACKNOWLEDGMENTS

This book would not have been possible without the intellectual and emotional support of my wife, Kathleen Frumkin, whose eye and ear for political outrages and linguistic nuances have informed this work throughout.

Editors are usually anonymous, but Eric Chinski deserves special mention. This book was written at his suggestion, and he slogged through many drafts, not just helping with the prose and organization but also catching dozens of places where ideas needed to be elaborated.

I especially celebrate the staff and interns of the Rockridge Institute for intellectual stimulation of the highest order: David Brodwin, Kenton de Kirby, Marc Ettlinger, Hilary Hammell, Thomas Hughes, Dan Kurtz, Terry Leach, Erik Sahlin, Anat Shenker-Osorio, Jessica Stites, Nancy Urban, and Alyssa Wulf. Chapter 7 draws on observations by Nancy Urban and Alyssa Wulf on interconnectedness and complex causation in environmental discourse. Marc Ettlinger also worked as my research assistant at the University of California.

Arianna Siegel and Sherry Reson have helped keep my life in order.

I also celebrate the Neural Theory of Language Group at the International Cognitive Science Institute, especially Ben Bergen, John Bryant, Nancy Chang, Ellen Dodge, Jerry Feldman, Olya Gurevich, Shweta Narayan, and Srini Narayanan.

Vittorio Gallese, friend and coauthor, took me through the details of mirror neuron research and helped me understand how frames could be physically embodied.

Mark Johnson, my colleague for more than twenty-five years, helped enormously when I needed his help.

I cannot say enough about how Peter Teague has helped over the years discussing topics on framing.

Joan Blades, Wes Boyd, Don Hazen, Markos Moulitsos, and Glenn Smith have been supportive throughout.

Steve Silberstein has been a friend and inspiration in all this work.

My son, Andy Lakoff, keeps teaching me new ways to think.

My brother, Sandy Lakoff, keeps filling me in on what has been thought before.

I have been blessed to be able to teach at the University of California at Berkeley for more than thirty years. My students have always been extraordinarily stimulating—challenging, asking tough questions, teaching me in innumerable ways. I thank them all. My colleagues there astonish me with what they know and the new knowledge they have created. I hope to keep learning from them.

Financial support for this project came partly from the Rockridge Institute and partly from the Richard and Rhoda Goldman Fund during my stint in 2004–2005 as Richard and Rhoda Goldman Distinguished Professor of Cognitive Science and Linguistics at the University of California at Berkeley.

Over the past several years, I have been fortunate to work with members of hundreds of advocacy groups, to learn from political leaders in the House and Senate and in the California legislature and from their staff members, to speak regularly with political journalists, to get to know deeply dedicated and knowledgeable members of the remarkable community of donors to political campaigns and advocacy groups, to work with leaders in the religious and scientific communities, and especially to encounter and converse with the thousands of people who have been kind enough to come to hear me speak and pepper me with questions. If there is any wisdom in this book, it has come from those encounters.

Berkeley, CA
January 31, 2006